STUDIES IN CONTEMPORARY SOCIO-ECONOMIC AND EDUCATIONAL PROBLEMS IN THE DEVELOPING WORLD: NIGERIA AS A CASE STUDY

STUDIES IN CONTEMPORARY SOCIO-ECONOMIC AND EDUCATIONAL PROBLEMS IN THE DEVELOPING WORLD: NIGERIA AS A CASE STUDY

JANET OLUSI, PH.D.,
ASSOCIATE PROFESSOR, ECONOMICS

S. V. KOBIOWU, PH.D.,
ASSOCIATE PROFESSOR,
SOCIOLOGY OF EDUCATION

iUniverse, Inc.
New York Lincoln Shanghai

STUDIES IN CONTEMPORARY SOCIO-ECONOMIC AND
EDUCATIONAL PROBLEMS IN THE DEVELOPING WORLD:
NIGERIA AS A CASE STUDY

iUniverse books may be ordered through booksellers or by contacting:

iUniverse
2021 Pine Lake Road, Suite 100
Lincoln, NE 68512
www.iuniverse.com
1-800-Authors (1-800-288-4677)

Because of the dynamic nature of the Internet, any Web addresses
or links contained in this book may have changed
since publication and may no longer be valid.

ISBN: 978-0-595-47781-4 (pbk)
ISBN: 978-0-595-60025-0 (ebk)

Printed in the United States of America

CONTENTS

FOREWORD

This book bas been written primarily for students, both in secondary and tertiary institutions. It is also useful for professional people, and the general reader, who are interested in being informed about the socio-economic and educational problems bedeviling the developing world. It is common knowledge that since the contributors are participant observers, they are armed with first hand information, which is being disseminated to the world at large, through this medium.

This effort has been motivated by the need to provide guided material in the areas of socio-economic and educational domains in the contemporary developing world. Although, the focus though appears wide and unwieldy, this book has been tailored in a way that it should arouse, stimulate, captivate and sustain the interest of the reader.

The varied chapters presented, after peer review, were later edited by Dr Janet Olusi, of the Department of Economics, and Dr S. V Kobiowu, of the Department of Educational Foundations and Counseling, both of the Obafemi Awolowo University, Ile-Ife, Nigeria

We commend this authoritative book to all who are interested in being informed about the socio-economic and educational problems that plague the developing world.

EDITORS

Professor Janet Olusi whose Professorship was announced on the 20th of November 2007, is in the Department of Economics, Obafemi Awolowo University, Ile-Ife, Nigeria.

She is in the area of Development Economics, with greater interest in gender factors in development, especially in agricultural development. She is equally interested in current economic issues, like economic deregulation, AIDS, and its impact on the economy. She has published in both national and international journals. Some of these include: "Environmental Impact of Having Women's Resources Control in Nigeria" "Economic Policy Reforms and Environment, Nairobi, Kenya; Enhancing Female Participation in African Agricultural Transformation in ISSUE, Birmingham; and Impact of Socio-economic Factors on Agricultural Development, Scandinavia Journal of Development Alternative., Sweden. She has traveled far and wide, and belongs to many International Organizations.

Dr S.V. Kobiowu is an Associate Professor in Sociology of Education at the Obafemi Awolowo University, Ile-Ife. Nigeria. He joined the then University of Ife, now Obafemi Awolowo University, in 1981, as a Graduate Assistant, and attained the present status in 1996.

He has continued to be productive and professionally active as a teacher, researcher, and an administrator. He has authored a number of books, and contributed to a number of others, apart from subscribing to a number of internationally recognized and reputable local journals.

His area of specialization is Sociology of Education. He has made contribution to knowledge in the area of the study of such societal structures that enhance the harmonious functioning of the society, by ensuring societal cohesion and conformity. He has also contributed considerably, through his research, to the awareness that there is need for consensus, rather than conflict in society, as no society can make any meaningful progress in a state of tension and animosity.

He has made valuable contributions to the intellectual, administrative and social life of the university, as well as the larger community outside the university. He had served for a number of years as the Acting Head of his Department. He had also served as a member of the Faculty of Education Board of Studies, Faculty Postgraduate Committee, Faculty Review Panel, and the Board of Postgraduate College.

NOTES ON CONTRIBUTORS

Dr S.V. Kobiowu is an Associate Professor in the Department of Educational Foundations and Counseling, Obafemi Awolowo University, Ile-Ife. Nigeria. He is in the area of Sociology of Education. He has published research papers extensively, in both National and International journals, including the Perceptual Motor Skills, and the World Council for Curriculum and Instruction. He has also published a number of books, in addition to contributing a number of chapters to others. He is the Secretary of Ife Society of Educators.

Dr Olutoyin Dibu-Ojerinde is in the area of Tests and Measurement. She joined the university in 1982 as a Graduate Assistant, and is presently a Senior Lecturer, a status she attained in 1966. She has co0authored a number of books, and has published research papers in reputable National and International Journals.

She is an Editorial Consultant of a National Journal, and also an Associate Editor of an International Journal.

Dr Yetunde Ajibade is a Lecturer in the Department of Special Education and Curriculum Studies, Obafemi Awolowo University, Ile-Ife. Nigeria. She started her teaching career in Instructional Strategies, Language Education, and Curriculum Development in 1983. She has written extensively on Language teaching and Learning, in Journals and books. She is a member of Ife School Curriculum Improvement Group. She pioneered the establishment of a Language Development Center in Nigeria, where she resides.

Dr Oloyede Ezekiel Ojo teaches courses in Mathematics Education and Curriculum Studies in the Faculty of Education, Obafemi Awolowo University, Ile-Ife. Nigeria. He obtained his B. Sc Degree in Education/Mathematics, M.A. and Ph. D Degrees in Curriculum Studies (Mathematics), from the same university. His research interest centers on the use of culturally relevant materials in the teaching of mathematics to the Nigerian child. He is a member of Ife School Curriculum Improvement Group, as well as the Mathematics Association of Nigeria.

Dr I.O. Aransi is a Senior Lecturer in the Department of Local Government Studies, Obafemi Awolowo University, Ile-Ife, Nigeria. He holds a Bachelor of Arts/Education Degree from the University of Ife, now Obafemi Awolowo University, Ile-Ife, Nigeria. He obtained a Master of Public Administration Degree from the same University. In addition, he holds a Master of Science Degree in Political science from the University of Ibadan, Nigeria. He also obtained a Doctor of philosophy degree in Political Science from the University of Ibadan, Nigeria. He has to his credit many publications, including contribution to books, and several articles published in national and international journals.

Dr Clement S. Oni obtained his Ph.D at the University of Akron, Akron Ohio, U.S.A. He specialized in Vocational Technical Education. He joined the service of Obafemi Awolowo University, Department of Continuing Education in 1988, as Lecturer Grade II, and presently a Senior Lecturer, since 1996.

He has published in reputable journals locally, nationally and internationally. He has also contributed to a number of books published locally and internationally. He is an editorial member of some National Journals, consulting editor to some local journals, and an Editorial Board Member of two of the Faculty of Education, Obafemi Awolowo Academic Journals.

Mr. David A. Osuntogun is a Lecturer in the Department of Continuing Education, Obafemi Awolowo University, Ile-Ife, Nigeria. He specialized in Home Economics/Education from Indiana State University, Terre Haute, Indiana. U.S.A. He has published widely, both in Local, as well as International journals. He is presently teaching courses in Adult Education in the University.

Dr J.O. Akande is a Lecturer in the Department of Adult Education, Obafemi Awolowo University, Ile-Ife. Nigeria. His areas of specialization include Adult Education, Community Education, and Development. He has published widely in reputable Local and International Journals. He is a member of Nigerian National Council of Adult Education (NNCAE) and Ife School Curriculum Improvement Group.

Dr Joel Adeyanju is an associate Professor, in the area of Art and Educational Technology, at the Faculty of Education, Obafemi Awolowo University, Ile-Ife. Nigeria. He had been in the services of the university for more than twenty years. He has published extensively in National as well as International Journals. He has written a number of books, and has co-authored a number of others. He uses locally developed instructional materials to enrich his teaching.

Mr P.S Ogedengbe holds a B. Sc and M. Sc Degrees in Estate Management. He also holds a Master's Degree in Business Administration. He is presently a Lecturer at the Obafemi Awolowo University, Ile-Ife. Nigeria. He has also published a number of articles in reputable journals, both locally, as well as overseas.

Dr Janet Olusi is an Associate Professor in the Department of Economics, Obafemi Awolowo University, Ile-Ife. Nigeria. She is in the area of Development Economics, with special focus on gender factors, especially as they relate to agricultural development. She has published extensively in local, national, as well as international journals. She has also traveled extensively round the world, attending learned conferences. She belongs to a number of International Associations, among which are: International Association for Feminist Economics (IAFFE), Association of African Women for Research and Development (AAWORD), and Nigeria Economic Society.

CHAPTER ONE

THE CONCEPT OF SOCIAL PROBLEM

DR S.V. KOBIOWU

The most generally accepted definition of a social problem is that which portrays it as 'a situation', which is perceived by some group, as a source of dissatisfaction for its members, and in which preferable alternatives are organized, so that the group, or individuals in the group, are motivated to effect some change. The problem is social, because it has its origin among people, who are disturbed by its presence, and therefore yearn for a 'change'.

This definition presupposes the idea of a normal and desirable situation, and the most apt way of seeing social problem is that, society desires an improvement on a condition which violates an accepted value, and therefore must either be eliminated, resolved, or remedied, through collective action. In looking at this definition therefore, one could easily state that a social problem varies from society to society, and from time to time, within the same society. It also varies from person to person. There is a myriad of social problems confronting different societies, particularly developing countries, in an attempt to modernize. Some of these problems are fallouts of the modernization process itself. In practice, transition from traditional stage to modernity gives rise to a host of daunting socio-economic cum-political problems, which should be treated as part and parcel of the modernization process.

Social problems have both objective and subjective under-pining. The objective connotation is the condition itself, while the subjective is the belief that the situation would change. According to Julian, this had to do with evolution of societal values. The structural functionalists, typified by Merton (1968) and

Nisbet (1969), contended that a social problem exists wherever there is a significant discrepancy between social standard, and social reality. This discrepancy becomes manifest, when one or more of society's needs are not met, or when their realizations are threatened. Social problems are usually not accidental, they are deep-rooted in the society, which must have neglected the provision of certain basic needs. Social problems are nothing other than disruptions of the expected standards, which may threaten the fabric of the society.

Some of the examples of social problems, particularly within the school setting, and the society at large, include truancy, alcoholism, prostitution, drug abuse, poverty, mental problem, violence, prejudices, homosexuality, and broken homes. The degree to which these are problematic varies according to society, as mentioned earlier. All the behaviors that are labeled as social problems are considered anti-social, and therefore deviant. These are behaviors that are harmful to the society, and which the people want remedied, Munaie et al (1999)

Sociological concern for social problem, stems from its preoccupation with order in the society. It is not concerned with fragments, rather it is concerned with the totality of society, and it views society as a double-edged sword, that cuts both ways. The extent to which social problems encourage change, disturb the social organism, or help to modify the direction of change or dynamics of society, are the concerns of sociology. It is with this inclination that sociologists have evolved a number of techniques, with which to analyze and understand social problems, prominent among the techniques are:

* conflict model or alienation model;
* structural functional model or consensus model; and
* symbolic-interactionist approach.

CONFLICT MODEL

Conflict theorists are considered pessimistic in the short run, because they tend to view the existing problem as resistant to change, and they hold the view that efforts at reform, are futile.

There is no one dimension to the study of social problems, as some social problems may result from a number of sources, which are specific. Some may not be traceable to any source, since society is made up of people of diverse experiences and orientations. The nature of problems encountered, vary by group, and experience. Our attitude to a problem may be influenced by our position, experience, and income in the society.

CONSENSUS MODEL

The model contends that social problems are "what the people think they are". It constitutes situations which are perceived by some group as a source of dissatisfaction by its members, and to which alternatives are preferred, so that the group or individuals in the group are motivated to effect a change. This model has a prescribed way of behavior. It defines what is right, and wrong. The existence of social problems therefore, is traceable to the failure of the social system to conform with, the social standard. In finding solution to social problems, the structuralist feels that society needs overhauling. It is also argued that society must establish processes of rewards and punishment, for compliance and non-compliance, with societal expectations. It is therefore pertinent to trace the sources of social problems, which often include the individuals and family, deviant subcultures, or defiant socialization, further back. In this school of thought, societies have built in self-correcting tendencies.

Also, the alienation explanation is compatible with the consensus model. However, the conflict model traces the genesis of social problems to basic contradictions in the social system. Implicit in the alienation model is that, problems occur, because the privileged are disinclined to effect a change.

The various perspectives that have been used for the study of social problems are: social disorganization, value conflict, social pathology, deviant behavior, and labeling. These five perspectives have different definitions, causes, conditions, consequences and solutions.

Social disorganization perspective, simply refers to a situation of anarchy, or culture conflict. The causes of this lie in rapid social change, such that the order in the society is lost, and some sort of disharmony sets in. And in a bid to solve the problems that result from these factors, the society must equilibrate the constituent parts of the social organism, or in the alternative, slow down the application of technology to societal needs. The other area of dissatisfaction is that of value conflict. Some conditions may arise that are inconsistent or incompatible with the values of the society. Conflict of value is a major cause of this, and it could result from serious competition among groups or individuals that are gunning for the same thing. This situation cannot be resolved by anybody without recourse to consensus among members.

Also Social Pathological perspective is defined as a violation of moral expectations, caused by defective or ineffective socialization processes. The consequences of this include the dehumanization of the person. In order to provide solution, effort should be geared towards intensifying moral education.

The fourth one is that of Deviant Behavior. Deviant behavior is antisocial or departure from what is considered normal. There are several dimensions to this. An individual may become deviant as a result of his innate inability to conform to societal standards. The consequences of this situation are many, but again, it depends on the nature of the deviant group, in terms of its organization, goal and resources, and to really redeem the erring individuals, a process of re-socialization becomes essential. This could be done if there is a well-defined goal for the larger society. Society must rehabilitate the straying person into the fold, by stressing legitimate means and goals.

The fifth perspective of social problem is Labeling. Society has mechanisms by which more social problems are inadvertently created. Labeling a person as a criminal results in the social stratification of that person, which consequence might be to drive him further into the world of crime. To be able to label an act as deviant, the labeler must be aware of it, and if he succeeds in labeling, he may gain some recognition.

It could be seen that there is no single way of perceiving social problems. There are several types, and consequently, they present several facets. They all constitute disturbance to the social structure.

CHAPTER TWO

TRUANCY IN SCHOOL AS A SOCIAL PROBLEM

DR. S.V. KOBIOWU AND DR E.O. OLOYEDE

One of the social problems one will like to discuss is truancy, and it is pertinent to know who is a truant? According to the Advanced Learners English Dictionary, a truant is defined as one who begs, without justification, a vagabond, an idle rogue, in fact, a lay-about. A lazy idle person, who absents himself/herself from school without leave, one who wonders from an appointment place, or someone who neglects his/her duty post, or business.

The term truancy, when narrowly defined, applies to unjustifiable absence from school, without the parents' knowledge, or approval. Absence of course, in a rare occasion is justified, as when there is physical illness, which makes it very unwise for the concerned individual to be at school. Truancy means absenting oneself without an acceptable reason, whether or not the parents know and approve of it.

In its advanced stage, it is regarded as absenteeism among workers. The clinical view of truancy is that of staying off school, as one of several kinds of anti social behaviors. The association between truancy and other anti social conducts in girls, for example, is well established. Yet, we can say that the problem of truancy is almost as frequent in girls as in boys.

Today, government and individuals are fully aware, but sound education is a precondition for rapid, social, economic, political, cultural and technological development, and emancipation of a developing nation. And if this practice persists among our secondary school students, who are perceived as leaders of tomorrow, they would never achieve the objective of becoming future leaders in science and technology, among other areas.

To achieve these lofty goals, proper attention must be given to the unraveling of the root cause of truancy in our school. This leads us to the causes of truancy.

As in the common parlance, "there is no smoke without fire", for whatever wrong thing that happens, something must have been responsible for it. The case of truancy among our secondary school students is no exception.

Below are some of the causes alluded to, for rampant cases of truancy among our students, which can be conceptualized from the following angles: their family background/the parents, the students themselves, the peer group, and the teachers. Others include the facilities in the schools, government policy, and the societal attitude.

FAMILY BACKGROUND

This is one of the causes of truancy, as well as other social problems, and other related poor activities and demeanors among secondary school students. From the available information, truants are drawn disproportionately from lower class families-the poor families.

Families that cannot provide the required textbooks, writing materials, school uniforms, pocket money, and school fees, would have their children frequently sent away from school. The students with tattered clothes, or the ones that left home in the morning without food, or those owing schools fees, or those who do not have any writing materials, would not be expected to be in the class always.

Many things may be responsible for this kind of situation, some of which may include broken home, through divorce. Since there could no longer be collective care for the students; real poverty may also be responsible, the family may be unable to live above poverty line, the result of all these bounce back on their offspring.

Also, students with criminal parents and delinquent siblings, who would have had related deviant biological inheritance, in which case, breaking of rules and regulations is not regarded as an offence, or a spectacular thing to them, since they have learnt that from their parents. Because of this bad training, they leave home when they like, they never bother what good things they could get from school. Consequently, they go to the school, when they feel like going, and stay away from school when it catches their fancy.

STUDENTS

It is discovered that students with low intelligence, and low attainment level, tend to absent themselves frequently from school, to save them from the embarrassment they might have from their teachers and classmates. A student, who comes to the school today, and is asked a question that he/she could not answer adequately, may decide to engage in truancy from school, to escape what he regards as avoidable ridicule.

Investigation has also shown that majority of the students found staying away from schools most of the time, are identified as those suffering from neurotic tendency, that is, having neurotic disorders. It is clear from this same source that many problems of truancy, and other disorders are frequently associated with this problem, especially in boys. Students that have been having hard time, and bad experiences with their parents, on issues that relate to family ties, may develop a cold attitude and apathy toward other things, for the rest of the day. This may prevent such students from attending classes.

Personal ability of the students, among others, can cause inferiority complex, and if they are the brilliant ones, superiority complex equally occurs. The weaker students, as earlier stated, because of shame, may refuse to attend class regularly, and the good ones may not see good enough reason in attending class always. They may see this as a waste of their time.

Whenever students develop hatred toward their teachers, or their teaching methods, such students may not be interested in coming regularly to such classes, in order to avoid having things to do with such teachers.

SCHOOL

The school cannot be exonerated from the cause of truancy, and poor activities among secondary school students. It is still uncertain to what extent such factors within the school contribute to the problem of truancy.

According to Reynolds's investigation, school variables show significant determinants of absenteeism. The atmospheric condition of such environment, as well as discipline, coupled with the established rules and regulations governing the school, determine to a large extent, the type of school anyone attends.

The schools where the heads could not maintain proper discipline, such schools are bound to record substantive cases of truancy among the students. When they know that if they do not attend school regularly, nothing would happen to them, or that their constant absenteeism would not affect them in any way. As well all know, 'there is no sin in the town without laws'.

Once there is breakdown of rules and regulations, due to the insensitivity of the head, everybody would resort to what he/she likes.

GOVERNMENT

The government also has its own share of the blame. At a time, there was a government order that corporal punishment should no longer be used in our schools. Students on hearing this started taking laws into their hands. They resorted to coming to school only when it pleases them. The continuous assessment arrangement in a way also craves way for truancy. Once students have attempted their tests, they do not come to school regularly again.

Government delay in the payment of teachers' salary, and other incentives, has also contributed in no small measure, to the frequent strikes and closure of schools, which has almost 'killed' the interest of student in schooling. Because of incessant strikes, students have developed cold attitude toward schooling. So, they come to school when they like, as they are not even sure whether the school will be on, or off.

Failure on the part of the government to provide equipment and materials for the schools make teaching/learning environment no longer conducive for learning. Some classes are so overcrowded, particularly schools in big cities, such that students cannot even hear or understand whatever they are being taught. Some school building roofs are leaking, and when the rains are falling, such become un-conducive to learning.

From the aforementioned causes of truancy, it is necessary to discuss some of the effects. Truancy in its own perspective can be associated with poor performance, and low grades. Truants may remain absent from school because of a felt inability to succeed. In any event, truancy removes the students from school, and this makes learning virtually impossible for such students. Truancy results from a combination of factors, including alienation from school life.

The incidence of armed robbery on our highways in Nigeria, as elsewhere, may be comparable with many other nations throughout the world, where extremism of all sorts is almost becoming the norm. It is indeed very sad to note that Nigeria has recovered a relatively large number of criminals in foreign prisons. The basis could be traced in part to truancy in school. The aftermath of this act by such students is poor performance in their examination. Students that have not been constant in school, would not know what has been taught, and thus many not pass when faced with a test. Out of sight is out of mind, the saying goes. It is what you see that you perceive. It is what you perceive, if asked, that you will remember to explain. This leads to examination malpractices and several examination irregularities. Many nations, if not most nations, place high premium on paper qualification (certificate), otherwise referred to as credentialism. It is seen as a ticket, or passport to a great height. A dropout before the completion of his course liable to join a criminal group, to make both ends meet.

Frustration is what usually ends the life of truants, since they end up with no worthwhile things to do with their lives, other than to stay idle, and roam the street in search of non-existent jobs, with their half-baked certificates, if any at all. Students that had been consistently absenting themselves in their school work, and who managed to secure admission into higher institution of learning, either by default, or through one error of omission, or commission, may still continue in their usual old habits. A persistent truant almost remains the same, through his/her adult life, which will in turn reflect in his/her later working life, and achievement.

SOLUTION

There is no problem without a solution, truancy as a social problem can be eradicated by adopting the following strategies: every student is a unique personality, but no teacher can respond simultaneously in 35 or 41 different ways. Fortunately, there are certain positive actions and attitudes that teachers, parents, government, school and other agencies that contribute to the problem of truancy, and poor activities among secondary school students, can do to help the individual, no matter what his/her special problem is. Everyone needs love, confidence in his/her abilities, opportunities to serve others, and social acceptance. The teachers can take steps to see that their students' needs are met, and that their students receive their full attention. Teachers should vary their teaching methods, master their subject matter well enough, so that students would always be attracted to the school. Love is being advocated as a way of combating truancy, because education experts recognize the role of affective domain in imparting knowledge. Corporal punishment is not officially allowed in some parts of the country, even though some teachers still apply it. But even if it is allowed, it should be applied with caution. Otherwise, there is the tendency of turning the affected pupils into hardened rule breakers, in this case, hardened truants.

Teachers must maintain an accepting and emotionally stable atmosphere in the classroom. Once again, the need to embrace, understand, and accept school norms, should be encouraged by the teacher.

The teacher must also help the students to develop positive self-concept. Enough guidance and counseling programs should be organized for the students in school. Assessment, measurement, and evaluation of the students work must be done, to make reasonable judgement, regarding their performance and attendance in the class. Schools should be made attractive and interesting to the pupils.

Exchange of visits by the parents and teachers should be intensified. The teachers should visit the school, both to meet and exchange ideas on students' problems.

On the part of the parents, they should provide for the needs of their children, so that they will love to go to school. Parents should monitor the school-work, and activities of their children at home, and live a good exemplary life. Parents should feed their children well. Parents are to warn their children of the danger of moving with bad group. Charity, they say, begins at home. Parents should serve as model for their children, so that they may adjust well into whatever community they find themselves.

Schools should maintain discipline. Any student that violates the school rules and regulations should be made to face the music, to serve as a deterrent to others. In doing this, intending truants in the school will check themselves, and the cases of truancy and poor activities among secondary schools students would be reduced. The cooperation of the parents/teachers association should be put in place, to jointly monitor the activities of students.

Facilities should be equally provided, to make the school attractive to the students. Government, on its part, should be ready to provide equipment, facilities and materials that can make learning and teaching more effective in schools. Teachers' salaries should be paid, as at when due. This is to put an end to the incessant strikes and lockouts, thereby enabling them to concentrate fully on the academic work, to the benefit of the students, and the society at large.

Government should intensify the efforts of the inspectorate division, and the inspectors should move round the schools, with a view to ensuring that the teachers are doing what they are engaged to do.

CHAPTER THREE

CHILD ABUSE AS A SOCIAL PROBLEM

DR. S.V. KOBIOWU

INTRODUCTION

The institution of marriage brings two consenting adults together, for the purpose of companionship, sexual regulation, and in many cases for the purpose of producing children, particularly in the African society, of which Nigeria is a prominent constituent. When the children start coming, it is necessary for the parents to take care of them, from the helpless state in which they come into the world, till they will be in a position to fend for themselves. The act of taking care of children is very cumbersome, and entails the use of foresight. Since babies cannot talk, parents are in a situation of guessing what they want, at a particular point in time. All children require that their basic needs be met. How these are met, what values adult place on children, the amount of discipline administered, and how responsibilities are given-all these aspects of child-care are managed differently in different communities.

Parent—Child relationship

Many years back the parent-child relationship was very fragile, children were seen as miniature adults, and character training was the dominant concern. These days, children are no longer seen from adult point of view only, fundamental changes, which are affecting society, are in turn influencing child-care norms. Child-care experts are no longer dogmatic when giving advise, parents are encouraged to understand each child, and to trust their own feeling in relation to that child. Physically handicapped and mentally retarded children often require a great deal of attention, compared to the normal ones. The first social learning of a child occurs at home. His earliest experiences with his family, particularly with the mother, are important in determining his attitude towards and expectations of other individuals. The mother gratifies the child's primary needs for food, for alleviation of pain, and for warmth. As time goes on, the mother's presence becomes associated with the satisfaction of needs. She is seen as the source of pleasure, contentment and relief of tension. As such, the child soon learns to search for, and reach out to his mother, whenever he or she is hungry, in pain or uncomfortable. If the mother is nurturant and gratifies the child's needs promptly, and effectively, the child will develop favorable social attitudes. He will not hesitate to approach other people whenever the need arises, and will respond to others in a friendly manner. In a nutshell, the child's interactions with the mother form the bases for his reactions towards others (Lindsay, 1971). The interaction between a child and the mother lays the groundwork of the child's development of a sense of trust, or distrust in his encounter with fellow human beings in later life. Rewarding and gratifying experiences with the mother, makes the child to trust her, and by implication, others. In contrast, a mother who is not dependable, or does not attend to the child's needs satisfactorily, produces a sense of distrust of herself, and by implication, and extension, of others in the world.

Effect of the Economy on Family

Millions of children are living and growing up under economic, social and psychological conditions, which hinder their optimum development. Their problems are pointers to the fact that something is wrong with their pattern of interaction, their parents, or the neighborhood in which they live, or in which they grew up. Many children experience other forms of substitute care, like guardianship, fostering, or even adoption, in place of parental care. The parental surrogates, assumes responsibility for the child, but denies the opportunity for an on-going personal relationship with the actual parent, or the guardian. Some parents are immature, and overwhelmed with new or over-demanding responsibilities of child rearing. Others are poorly equipped with the knowledge, needed to give care to children, and maintain family balance. The consequence of these is gross child neglect. Many children run away from their homes, and migrate to cities, to live among others like themselves. Some do this as a way of escaping from inadequate, or lack of care from parents and caretakers, while others seek independence, individuality, or adventure, away from what to them, appear as no longer worthwhile environment. To many teenagers the open alternative is delinquency, which is compounded by the inadequate treatment and rehabilitative resources available, World Health Organization (1993).

Delinquency has both a cultural and legal basis, and may be viewed as the existence of conflict between the norms of society and conduct of an individual (Duseck, 1970). Some cases of delinquency may reflect in improper socialization, or child neglect, while others could be induced by environmental circumstances.

The vast majority of delinquents came from poor families, living in deteriorating or economically deprived neighborhoods, usually become delinquent. It is therefore obvious that socio-economic factors are not the only significant antecedents of delinquency. Personal insecurities, neglect and psychological problems, stemming from disturbed family relationships, may also be inherent in the delinquent's background.

In all societies, the act of reproduction is carried out to ensure the perpetuation of mankind. The passage from childhood to adulthood is one accompanied by the process of socialization, and parents are responsible for affecting this process. Socialization as a process involves inculcating the norms and values of the society into the young ones, coupled with taking care of them socially, morally, financially, or some combination. Socialization is therefore part and parcel of child-care, but some parents fail in this task. As such, their children suffer neglect in one form or the other. Children that are neglected go through a kind of socio-psychological trauma, and have problems fitting into the society. As a result of the unfavorable circumstances that avail themselves to the neglected child, he or she feels insecure. Hence, on attaining teenage status may start to deviate from the culture of the society. Teenagers who deviate from the culture of the society are referred to as delinquents. Delinquency could therefore be seen as a social term, which denotes law breaking, by persons not considered as adults.

Acts engaged in by delinquents are considered as immoral, or better still, anti-social, but varies with time, and from one place to another. Some of such acts are illegal, and formally sanctioned. Such include gambling, drug addiction, and trafficking, and even unlawful entry, while others are legal and hence, informally sanctioned. They include drinking alcohol, truancy and rudeness to elderly people. There is a link between child neglect and delinquent tendencies. Furthermore, delinquency has been increasing at an alarming rate recently. This is a threat to norms and values. Hence, society is faced with a problem. In combating delinquency therefore, the attempt should be such which aims at alleviating, or reducing the incidence of child neglect, before attention is given to other possible causes of delinquency.

CHAPTER FOUR

EXAMINATION MALPRACTICES AS A SOCIAL PROBLEM IN NIGERIA

DR. S.V. KOBIOWU; DR MRS DIBU-OJERINDE
AND DR E. O. OLOYEDE

INTRODUCTION

An educational examination may be defined as the assessment of a person's performance, when confronted with a series of questions, problems or tasks, set him in order to ascertain the amount of knowledge that he has acquired, the extent to which he is able to utilize it, or the quality of, and effectiveness of the skills he has developed. Formal examinations, involving written answers to a series of prepared questions, were first used by the Chinese in the 2nd Century B.C., to select recruits for the Civil Service. Candidates were required to pass written examinations in literature and history, and also to demonstrate their proficiency in written poetry, in music and archery. Those who were successful had to take the examinations afresh every nine years, to retain their posts, and the highest official, the prime minister, was expected to prove that he was entitled to his superior rank, by competing regularly, and winning the highest place.

The Jesuits introduced written examination into their schools in the 16th Century. The definitive Ratio Atque Institution Studiorum of 1599, which was not revised until 1932, contains, a code of rules for the conduct of school examinations, which were held annually, and determined whether or not children were promoted to a higher class, or grade.

During the 19th century, formal written examinations became regular in universities, schools and other educational institutions. Examinations were also increasingly employed for the selection of recruits to the Civil Service, and the professions, and to posts in industry and commerce.

USES OF EXAMINATION

(a) **Evaluation of Progress:** Examination developed by the teachers to assess their pupils' progress must be as old as formal education itself, for they are an integral part of the profession of teaching. Although their main, and obviously essential purpose is to ascertain the amount of knowledge a pupil has retained, they also have other important roles. It is generally recognized that a pupil cannot be successfully educated, if he is required to assume a wholly passive role. He must be given the opportunity to practice his skills, if they are to be effectively developed, and to apply his knowledge, if it is to become systematically organized. Rarely can a teacher give his pupils incentive to work hard over a long period, without resorting to the use of tests, or examinations.

Regularly, assessments also enable teachers to furnish meaningful reports on the progress of pupils to the head of school, or to the head of another school, to which the pupil may transfer, to a prospective employer, or to the pupils' parents.

Another useful by-product of the procedure of assessment, or evaluation, is that it focuses the attention of teachers and pupils alike on the objectives they are jointly seeking to attain. If a teacher regularly sets examinations to tests his pupils' progress, he can scarcely avoid considering the ends for which his course of instruction has been designed.

The examination results will indicate how far these objectives are likely to be attained, and therefore, the extent to which they can be regarded as appropriate goals for the pupils.

(b) **Evaluation of Effectiveness of Instruction:** An examination that measures the performance of pupils may also be used to evaluate the effectiveness of the teacher, and the method he employs. A poor performance does not necessarily imply that a pupil is lacking in ability or application. Examinations are increasingly used to investigate the conditions in which successful learning takes place, to compare the effectiveness of different methods of teaching, to examine the influence on pupils progress of various forms of school organization, etc.

The tests may also be used to determine whether particular remedial reading instruction, as an example, depends to a marked degree, on the use of careful diagnostic testing procedures, followed by specific remedial procedures, adapted to the particular needs of the individual students. This selection of specific remedial procedures to meet the specific needs of each student is the basis of such programs.

(c) **Guidance:** In most modern schools, examinations serve a wider purpose than that of progress assessment alone. Two major developments during the 20th century have combined to transform the organization of educational systems, particularly within highly industrialized countries. First, the considerable accumulation of knowledge about individual differences in pupils' ability, and aptitude. Secondly, the technical advances that have increased the complexity of the process involved in the production and exchange of goods, to such an extent that society demand specialized training, knowledge and adaptability.

The allocation of pupils to appropriate educational courses is an important task, and a considerable amount of research is devoted to discovering suitable techniques for it. Tests and examinations designed to reveal the pattern of each pupil's abilities, aptitudes, attainments, and interests play an important part in these procedures.

(d) **Selection:** A complementary process to that of guidance is selection of individuals for a particular educational institution, or type of employment, while guidance involves determining the kind of education suited to a pupil's needs, and the type of subsequent employment will give scope to his aptitudes. Selection is used to determine which individuals will be admitted to particular educational institution, or particular employment, and in many countries, examinations are regularly used for this purpose.

Admission to course of higher education in universities and other institutions is frequently determined, at least in part, by examination results. Selection procedures, which include examinations, are also used to fill posts in the Civil Service, in the many branches of industry and commerce.

(e) **Certification:** Another important purpose of examination is to provide evidence that a person has achieved a specified standard of attainment.

Examinations at the end of a secondary school or University course, for example, certify that an individual has completed the course successfully. Examinations of this kind are also set by professional institutions, to determine whether or not a person should be regarded as a qualified member.

TYPES OF EXAMINATION

(1) **Written:** This is the type of examination that is used to test students' ability. It is administered to know a "good" student, and also to know how well a student can compose and present facts. Written examination can be done either in or outside the school institutions.

Oral examination is the type that makes students to face a group of people or panel, whereby such a student or students will be interrogated. This is usually done in English Language.

Practical examination is the type that makes students to make use of their brains and hands, and to undergo the practical aspects of the subjects that are written down. It is done on such subjects such as Biology, Chemistry, Physics and Agriculture.

(2) **Essay type and Objective Examination:** Essay type can be extended or restricted. It is easy to prepare, and it makes the examiner to know whether a student or students can express themselves well or not. Objective examination is part of essay type. It can be multiple choice, matching, true or false, short answers and completion forms. Majority of the subjects that are presented in the examinations, have both Essay and Objective types. Such as English Language, Biology, Chemistry, Physics, etc.

(3) **Internal and External Examinations:** Internal examinations are those that are done within the institutions of learning. This type of examination is being administered within the school system, in order to give teachers feedback, to decide the position of the students, to know students' weakness, and strengths, etc.

External examinations are those done outside the institution, e.g the one conducted by the West African Examinations Council (W.A.E.C). It is conducted to determine which student will go further in education, and which will take to another calling.

CONCEPT OF EXAMINATION MALPRACTICE

According to Encyclopedia Britannica (1769), the concept of malpractice is defined as dereliction from professional duty, whether intentional, criminal or merely negligent, by one rendering professional services, that results in injury, loss, or damage to the recipient of those services, or to those entitled to rely upon them, or that affect the public interest adversely.

Barnhant and Barnhant explain malpractices as criminal neglect, or wrong practice, or conduct, in any official or professional position, misconduct, etc.

TYPES OF EXAMINATION MALPRACTICES

Examination malpractice is not restricted to certain level of education, but rather it covers all levels, starting from primary school level to the tertiary institution. The types of examination malpractices can be broadly grouped into three parts.

Examination malpractice by the candidate himself/herself; examination malpractice being encouraged by teachers; and examination malpractice being encouraged by external forces.

(a) **Examination malpractices by candidates**
   * Copying from notes and textbooks;
   * Copying from other candidates;
   * Dictating points to themselves
   * Sitting for, and sitting for examinations for their friends.

(b) **Examination malpractice by teachers**
   * Working solutions on the chalkboard for the candidate, especially in Mathematical subjects such as Mathematics, Statistics, Chemistry, Physics, etc.
   * Helping students to get notes or script from one student to another, or from outside the examination hall to the examination hall.
   * Influencing marks by inflating marks.
   * Helping students to smuggle out 'life-questions' e.g. the examination that is expected to be conducted in about two or three days time, might have been treated before the examination day.
   * Helping students prepare ready-made solutions in answer script, during or after the examination.
   * Teacher also dictates solution to students in examination hall.

(c) **Examination Malpractice by External Forces**

The external forces we are talking about are the custodians of examination question papers, such as the examination officials (WAEC) officials, Bank officials, police officers, Education officers, Local Government officials, etc. These are done in the following ways.

* Smuggling out 'life question paper', before the examination day. This is done either to enrich their purse or to derive other material gains.
* Influencing marks, by altering the originally awarded marks by the examiners or markers.
* Change of already submitted answer scripts with newly prepared answer scripts.

CAUSES OF EXAMINATION MALPRACTICE

The students are lazy to read, and they are desperate to pass the examination by all means. As one realizes, examination is often times used to secure position (see the uses of examinations).

Teachers and the custodians of examination papers usually engage in such practices to enrich themselves, that is, for monetary gains. The importance attached to certificate in our society also propels the students to have it, by all means.

It is also done to win the opposite sex, that is, to satisfy their sexual urge.

Solutions to Examination Malpractices

The Federal Military Government of Nigeria on the 10th of May, 1999 promulgated Decree No. 33 on Examination Malpractices, for offences such as cheating at examinations; impersonation; disorderliness at examinations; disturbances at examinations; obstruction of supervisor; forgery of result slip; breach of duty and conspiracy, and aiding, among others. All aimed at stopping the malpractices. Despite the decree however, the situation continues unabated.

Examination malpractices have become a sore spot in the minds of many educationists, and successive governments. This has led to many steps being taken by many organizations, like the West African Examination Board and governments, to stem this ugly tide. Among other necessary steps to be taken, the following become imperative:

* Proper counseling should be given on examination malpractice, enlightening the students and the public on the immediate and the after-effect of the practice.
* Promulgation of further stiff penalty to the offenders, like as stated by Nigeria's Decree 20, which reads thus: Any person who fraudulently or with intent to cheat or secure any unfair advantage to himself, sells, and buys, or otherwise deals with any questions papers intended for the examination of persons at any examination, or commits any of the offences, shall be guilty of an offence, and on conviction sentenced to 21 years imprisonment.
* On the other hand, institutions like the West African Examination Councils, or other such related Examination Councils, tertiary institutions, etc. should also take the following steps, to stop examination malpractices.
* Withholding of results of those affected;
* Cancellation of results of those affected;
* Banning such students(s) and institution/s from taking the subsequent examinations, for a number of year(s);
* Suspension of such students from the institution of learning;
* Surcharging such students certain amount of the cost of re-conducting the examination again by the institution.

CONCLUSION

In conclusion, the effects of examination malpractices do not allow the nation, the individual, and corporate bodies, to grow in the right direction. For example, a medical student who engaged in examination malpractices during his training, and who "successfully" completes, only graduates to be killing patients, when he begins to practice the profession.

Furthermore, for a nation to grow, government should study, more rigorously, the causes of examination malpractices—students' laziness to read, influence of monetary gain, sexual urge, and such other petty and negative considerations. Government should also incorporate the solutions proffered in this essay, in addition to many others, and set up a committee to further study the malaise of examination malpractices, and deal decisively with the problem, thereby giving more credibility to the certificates that are awarded by the examining bodies.

CHAPTER FIVE

YOUTH DELINQUENCY

DR. S. V. KOBIOWU

INTRODUCTION

The youth period, which also encompasses the period of life between eleven to eighteen (11–18) years, is the period between childhood and adulthood. During this period, an individual experiences a lot of changes, not only physiologically, including the maturation of sexual organs, but also physically—the most rapid increase in height occurs at this time, as well as socially—the adolescent begins to interact with adults, responds like adults, and expects adult treatment. Also, this period is an emotional period of storm and stress.

CHARACTERISTICS OF THE ADOLESCENT PERIOD

As the definition above implies, the adolescent is in a transition between childhood and maturity. He is neither a child nor adult, but is caught in a field of over-lapping forces and expectations. His characterizing qualities are neither those of a child, nor those of adults. The adolescence period is also characterized by a rapid increase in body size and weight. For the girl, normal adult height is reached, while the boy may continue to grow up to the early twenties. The physical strength in boys is significantly increased, and if not properly channeled, the adolescent boy can get into problems.

The male notices a change in voice, develops hair characteristics, and the female ovulation cycle starts. These physical or physiological changes are concomitant with sexual excitements, and, or embarrassment. The adolescent, most often, seeks emancipation from parents or relevant authority.

JUVENILE DELINQUENCY AND DEVELOPMENTAL TASKS

The concept juvenile delinquency is multifarious and heterogeneous, ranging from personal, social, educational and vocational, to legal, political, moral, and religious problems. Some of those problems are discussed below.

PERSONAL PROBLEMS

These include physical appearance, self-assertion, worries about health, finances, transportation, etc. Every adolescent wants to be regarded as good-looking, strong individuals, and would do every thing to dress well. This is accompanied by rebellion, or self-assertion for independence from parents, and others in authority. The home no longer provides a model, and the adolescent starts to model peers and others outside the home. In short, the personal problems of the adolescent are increased when the home situation is unsatisfactory, or when the home is broken, as a result of death or divorce.

Emotions tend to heighten the adolescents' personal problems. These emotions are exaggerated, as the adolescent can swing from heightened euphoria of laughter, to depression within a very short period of time. Laughter can be quite loud for the slightest provocation. Managing personal problems spill over onto social problems, so it is rather difficult to draw a distinction between the tremendous problems facing the adolescent.

ADOLESCENTS' SOCIAL PROBLEMS

Some adolescents are early maturers, while others are late maturers. For an early maturing girl, a problem can be created for her age mates, while for the boy, an advantage may be gained. The girls' early development results in her being conspicuous, at a time when such is not valued, and can expose her to males. Many may find themselves embarrassingly tall. Over-weight, or having fully developed breasts than their age, can also cause problems. These initial disadvantages could give way to being socially advantageous, particularly by the time the girl enters the senior secondary school.

Boys who are physically more matured are usually accepted, and accorded leadership roles by peers, and are socially welcomed by adults. These boys can be appointed students leaders, and given prominent positions in athletics. The slow maturing boy is considered too immature to fix dates with girls of his own age, receives no leadership appointments, and frequently develops feelings of inferiority, which may persist for a life-time. Other adolescent social problems include drug abuse, and during the later adolescent period for girls marriage worries. The drugs commonly abused by the adolescents are antibiotics, tobacco, alcohol and marijuana, among others. The reasons for such abuse is usually for experimentation, pressures from peers, and an attempt to escape from the frustrations of the turbulent period.

EDUCATIONAL AND VOCATIONAL PROBLEMS

Adolescents face great problems adjusting to school-work. They spend little time studying, and worry excessively about examination. Some are afraid to speak in class, and lack interest in some subjects, such as mathematics, or physics, etc.

In addition, some teachers are feared by some adolescents, especially those who are viewed as rigid, conservative, and partial. If such teachers assign home work, the adolescent may refuse to do it, preferring to be idle in class, or even boycott schools.

Another significant problem area for the adolescent is the choice of vocation. The school, or the home provides initial assistance in this regard. So, the adolescent may choose an occupation, regardless of the relevant academic performance. The influencing factor for the choice of vocation may be for prestige, or the financial reward attached to the profession. For example, an adolescent may want to be a lawyer, or a medical doctor, because of the economic and social benefits enjoyed by these professions. Parents may want their youngsters to be part of the professions, which they themselves perhaps had wanted to be part of, but did not have the opportunity, accompanying attitude, and talents. Such parents are ill equipped to advise the adolescents properly. Consequently, an adolescent may choose a profession that may prove too tough academically, or non-challenging or satisfying.

The adolescent who destroys the school property, steals from fellow students, or commits minor juvenile offences, is punished by the school authority, or by the parents or guardian. For arson, the adolescent is tried by the juvenile court, and is sent to the remand homes. Thus, the adolescent is faced with legal identity problem, not receiving the benevolent childhood understanding by adults, or the harsh legal "hammer" for the adult offender.

MORAL OR RELIGIOUS PROBLEMS

The adolescent faces moral and religious problems. The adolescent finds an inconsistency between what he sees and what he has been told. He has listened to the adult preach good moral behavior on one hand, and behave as a "sugar daddy" on the other hand. He has also seen the adult embezzle public funds, and take bribes, while at the same time condemning these behaviors. People get rich over-night by stealing public funds, and being honored by their kinsmen, without anybody questioning the source. The adolescent, who has the full intellectual functioning as the adult, faces conflicting moral messages. This creates cognitive dissonance that must be resolved during this period. Adults condemn the adolescents' attempt to mate and co-habit with age mates. Pre marital sex is a taboo. At the same time, these adults are seen living together without being married, and engaging in immoral behavior. Again, the adolescent may disobey the parents, may want to stay away late from home, and in very severe cases, may run away from home completely.

In the present society, the traditional religious ways have broken down. The adolescent is exposed to a lot of religious systems. He lacks the experience of the adult to select his own religious group. This problem gets more complex when the adolescent has no strong religious exposure as a child. If care is not taken, the adolescent may never find a true solution to the religious problem, and may be vacillating between traditional religious experimentation (going to native juju men) and one form of established religious group or the other, throughout life.

The adolescent, in order to adapt into adult oriented behavior, and to fulfill his appropriate role without discontinuity, must master the problems stated below:

Havighurst (1952) outlined the developmental tasks that are very significant for the adolescent. These are:

* Achieving new and more mature relations with age mates of both sexes.
* Achieving a masculine or feminine social role.
* Accepting one's physique, and using the body effectively.
* Achieving a measure of economic independence.
* Achieving emotional independence of parents and other adults.
* Selecting and preparing for an occupation.

* Preparing for marriages and family life.
* Developing intellectual skills, and concepts, needed for assuming the duties and privileges of citizenship.
* Desiring and achieving socially responsible behaviors.
* Acquiring a set of value and ethical system as a guide to behavior.

Some of the ways by which the teacher can help the adolescent cope with their Problems include the following:
1. Achieving new and more mature relations with age mates of both sexes.
* Encouraging healthy, mature, and responsible relationship between members of same sex and opposite sex.
* Organizing activities like debating, drama, writers club, and other social activities for the young individuals.
* Sex education, and knowledge of dating practices.
* Teaching students respect for self, and others.
* Teaching students the dynamics of interpersonal relations.

2. **Achieving a masculine or feminine social role.**
    By assigning female or male role to students in the school. For example, making males prefects, for males, and female prefects for female students.
    Encouraging the teaching of students that stress different roles of both sexes. For example, home economics for females, and giving students responsibilities that would enable them to play masculine or female roles, both at home and in the school.

PREPARING FOR MARRIAGE AND FAMILY LIFE

Encouraging youth participation in the running of school and home affairs. Teaching youths responsibilities, finance and home management. Teaching them mutual trust and understanding for members of the same, as well as the opposite sex.

Developing intellectual skills and concepts necessary for civil competence.

Encouraging youth participation in youth organization, and other social welfare activities, and other extra curricular activities. Teaching of social sciences, and relating this subject to everyday life-happenings. Exposing youth to group work and shared-activities. Teaching youth to identify their civic rights, duties, obligations and responsibilities.

3. **DESIRING AND ACHIEVING SOCIALLY RESPONSIBLE BEHAVIORS**
    * Providing youth with necessary information, and educating them on proper/good manners, and etiquette.
    * Giving youth duty posts, which would enable them develop sense of responsibility. For example, making them prefects and members of some school committees.
    * Teaching youth the accepted norms and culture of the society they live in, and making them have knowledge of the responsibilities, demands, and limitations placed on them by their society.
    * By making teachers, counselors, parents and other authority figures act as good models to youth, so that they can learn socially accepted behaviors from them, and also learn about their limitations.

4. **Acquiring a Set of Values and Ethical System as a Guide to Behaviors**
    * Teachers and counselors, parents and other authority figures should act as good models to the youth, so that they can learn good values and ethical system.
    * Rewarding and commending positive value systems, exhibited by the youths.
    * Encouraging healthy relationships among members of their peer groups, especially healthy competition, and group work.
    * And lastly, but maybe, not exhaustively, non-imposition of adult values on youths, but guiding and leading them to develop, which must be in line with the accepted positive values of their society.

CHAPTER SIX

SECRET SOCIETIES AND CULTS IN SCHOOLS

DR. S. V. KOBIOWU

INTRODUCTION

In their innocence, ignorance or out of sheer folly, many students march straight into the jaws of death, in the hands of operators of secret societies and cults, flourishing in several institutions of higher learning. These associations and fraternities are wicked, extremely wicked. They are not just wicked to other people, they are even wicked to their members. There are reports about prospective cult members who die in the process of initiation rituals. Some members equally die as a result of internal clashes among members. Others die in circumstances that cannot be adequately understood by non-cult members. They die physically and spiritually.

Secret cults and societies commit unspeakable atrocities against other innocent students, injuring them, paralyzing them, and sometimes killing them out-rightly, in cold blood. They constitute themselves into a menace, destroying property belonging to other individuals, and in fact, public property. They are specialists in arson, rape, murder, vandalism and other atrocities. This is why in recent times, authorities have descended heavily on those nocturnal and subterranean organizations, known by the tag secret cult.

Perhaps, it is pertinent at this juncture to pause, and ask the question, 'What is a secret cult?' But the answer is not an easy one. Darul (1966), for instance gives two reasons why it has not been possible for scholars and writers to successfully provide a satisfactory definition of a secret cult. One, there are many variants surrounding the central fact of the existence of the society, that will identify one cult, and will not fit another. Secondly, not all secret societies are entirely secret. For instance, there are secret societies, whose members may be known, (as in the case of Freemasonians); or those whose objectives may be stated publicly, (as with the Rosicrucians, among others.

Nevertheless, we need a basic definition of a secret cult, for our purpose. There are some features associated with secret cults. These include: (a) exclusivity of membership: (b) the use of signs, passwords, and similar rather esoteric materials, group objective, and shared experience of rituals and beliefs, especially the myth of the society. For the purpose of this exercise, we will define a secret cult to mean any form of organization, whose activities are not only exclusively kept away from the knowledge of others, but such activities are carried out at odd hours of the day, and they often clash with the accepted norms and values of the society, (Ogunbameru, 1977).

One may begin to wonder who the members are. They are students like you. Incidentally, some lecturers fully cooperate with them, for reasons best known to hem. These associations are not legally registered. They operate under the cloak of darkness.

Now, one may ask, why do people join secret societies and cult? There are several reasons. Some of these reasons may include the following:

i.   People do different things for different reasons, so also is it with membership of discredited subterranean associations. People who join think they derive pleasure and satisfaction from doing so. Those who join these associations are operating under the chain of Satan.

ii. It takes the special grace of God to liberate them from their bondage. They do not realize that they are being oppressed and tormented. Satan makes it impossible for them to realize the fact. If they know, they would all run away from secret societies and cults.

How do people become members of secret societies and cults? The following are some of the ways they become members. These are membership by association, by experimentation, and by compulsion.

Let us examine them one after the other.

1.   A friend, colleague or associate, who is a member of such a society, can lure one into becoming a member. Even classmates in the same department, can lure one into becoming a member.

They can lure with a sugar-coated mouth, and through false words, meant to deceive would-be members. They will give what they feel is attractive. They will not tell the real aims and modus operandi of the association, but paint glamorous pictures of their aims and objectives. Whereas, behind this painted sepulcher is the cadaverous odor of souls, spirits and bodies destroyed. Rebuke them and stand firm. They are highly surreptitious. Be on your guard, because they will not go back immediately. They will insist, persist and press hard until you succumb, and fall headlong into the pit of death. Avoid them if you do not want to perish.

2. **Membership by experimentation is the next thing we shall discuss.**

Members secretly persuade other students to attend their meetings, by encouraging them form room to room. They achieve this objective by painting a rosy, and gentle picture of the set-up. They come up with such pretensions as: they have never insulted anybody before, they do not fight, injure or kill. Instead, they will boast that their association confers power on their members, and that their members, perform excellently in examinations, sports and social life. They dominate the students union, which you admire so well.

You may decide to attend their meeting only once to see for yourself, and know if the association is as bad as portrayed. If it is bad, you believe, you will never go there again. There you are! Next week you steal to the venue of the meeting, perhaps under the cover of night. We cannot explain what happens thereafter. But all we know is that you have become one of them.

That is one aspect of the problem. Another aspect is that some administrators and lecturers in higher institutions and even in secondary schools, and other higher institutions of learning, are members alongside their students. They have compromised their moral authority. They are neck-deep in varied shameful activities, so they do not want to be exposed. That is why they maintain an unholy, unquiet alliance and silence.

Some school authorities have succeeded in reducing the incidence to the barest minimum. There are others who are still trying their best. One thing that makes the struggle difficult is the fact that these organizations are unregistered. It is difficult to know who the members are, so it is not possible to hold specific persons responsible for collective inimical actions.

Theoretical Basis and the Way out

Organized crime is a secret conspiratorial activity that generally eludes and evades law enforcement. Organized crime is the work of a group that regulates relations between various criminal enterprises, involved such as in narcotics, prostitution and gambling. Organized crimes often serve as a means of mobility for individuals struggling to escape poverty. They have their groups, like the cocaine pushing group. It is during their secret meetings that they grouped themselves to the branches mentioned above. They also appear victimless in nature, (Elegbeleye, 1977).

Victimless crime implies, willing exchange among students of widely desired, but illegal goods and services. In contrast to white-collar or index crimes that endanger people's economic or personal well-being against their will, or without their direct knowledge, victimless crimes have no "victim" other than the offender. Secret cults and societies, gambling, prostitution, drunkenness and drug abuse are victimless crimes.

The major panacea that can curb the above quoted act could be attained through the effort of government, by waging war against secret cults and societies. The parents too could be another major panacea that can curb the act among the students. Parents should stop fraternizing with cults in their communities and societies.

School authorities can also wage war against secret cults and societies, through rustication of any student caught as one of the secret cult members. Not only that, the society can also curb their activities, by alienating, and if need be, even ostracizing those who are confirmed to be members of secret cults.

CHAPTER SEVEN

CRISIS IN EDUCATION IN NIGERIA

DR. S. V. KOBIOWU

INTRODUCTION

In talking about crisis in education, one needs to examine and understand the problem of inequalities. It is when there are comparisons, that valuations of judgement of relative worth arise, for if there is no diversification of privileges on the part of the constituent groups of society, there would not be room for comparisons.

In science, we are told that all living things possess many things in common, such as growing, feeding, respiration, excretion, etc., but with critical studies, it has been discovered that there are differences in the process. Plants respire differently from animal, and fish feeding is different from bird feeding; while human beings reproduce differently from other animals like reptiles, amphibians, and the apes, among others.

Public—Private Ownership of Schools in Nigeria

In Nigeria, like other countries, there are private schools, owned by different proprietors, individual or corporate groups, as well public/schools, which are owned by the government. The Private Schools put in a lot of effort, to see that they provide a relatively higher standard education, which would make many parents wish to send their children to such private schools. They would appoint competent teachers, and see that they are treated in a way that would make them work hard, in order to elevate the name of the school. Not that alone, they would see that the schools are supplied with all the necessary amenities, such as well ventilated classrooms, good and enough furniture, and appropriate instructional materials.

The government public schools are not so equally equipped, as the private schools. The government does not care much, regarding the proper/adequate staffing of many of the public schools under her jurisdiction. In some government owned schools, one can count about eighty and above pupils, assigned to just one teacher, whereas the classroom can only accommodate fifty pupils conveniently. Even though the recommended teacher-student ratio by UNESCO is 1:25. Most of the classrooms also are without good and enough furniture, not to talk of instructional materials. This indifference to the provision of amenities has laid the foundation for crisis in the classroom. One important thing that we should all be aware of, is that the youths of today are tomorrow's adults. And that every society should think of a well ordered obligation to its youth, an obligation to feed, clothe, educate and generally prepare them to inherit the earth and carry on, in comfort and relative peace and safety within God's vineyard. In every society, the youth represent a dream, a hope, and a future. They also represent fear and uncertainty. Both extremes determine and inform a society's attitude toward its youth. A society's dream is the sum total of its ambitions, and for it to realize and sustain these ambitions, it must first of all survive.

It is therefore, necessary for society to have the means of assuring itself that it can survive as an entity, and realize these ambitions, if not today, then tomorrow. Over the years the individuals, within government have formulated the educational policies for the nation. For example, in 1987, when Professor Jubril Aminu was the Education Minister, he effected a change of the school calendar, both in primary and secondary institutions. His major reason for the change to January—December from the existing September—June Calendar was that, it will afford farming parents help from their wards, in the peak harvest periods. Many may argue that having regard to Nigeria's different geographical climate zones, not to talk of dissimilarities of crop cycles, it is difficult to justify such, as responsible for a major adjustment in the educational policy of the country, as enunciated by Jubril Aminu's agricultural gospel.

When the January—December calendar that existed from colonial times was replaced in 1973, at least three compelling reasons were proffered. First, there was a felt need to synchronize the primary and post primary year with the tertiary institutions' session. A high school graduate in June, had a three months break, and thereafter walked straight into the tertiary institution, if successful. Three quarters of a year off academic work, could be a painful diversion. There was usually a considerable problem involved, in the subsequent mental re-turning to the classroom culture, for the few who were lucky enough, to keep the will for higher learning alive.

Secondly, for those who were yet to pass the required subjects, the holiday period between June and September was considered ample summer school preparatory session for the next class. The third reason was that all over the world, the September—June calendar had become the vogue. Professor Aminu felt so personally impressed with his new imposition, that he quite often considered any further discussion on the matter impertinent.

Instability in Government policies

Policies for formal education in Independent Nigeria, as elsewhere, and their implementation, have somewhat assumed a permanent state of flux, sometimes bizarre, and at other times, contradictory and unintelligible, to those who ought to understand their bases. Pupils who were affected by the change of the 1973–1974 academic year lost a term of studies. This time around, pupils who have been caught in the web of reversal to the Pre—1973 calendar, for example, were made to waste a term of studies, in the process of transiting from one segment of the education ladder to the other.

One significant educational policy embarked upon by Nigeria was the free Primary Education Scheme of the former Western Region, in 1955. This led to significant surge in the educational fortunes of the region. Even when the government that initiated the scheme was no longer in power, education in the region still remained free, and materials and manpower were provided adequately. But the year 1972 could be regarded as a watershed. While the free education program of 1955 was restricted to the Western Region, the decision of the Federal Government in 1972, that states should acquire all schools owned by missions, voluntary agencies, and individuals, affected the entire country's education. That decision, it seems, was based on nationalistic sentiments, that the education of the citizenry ought to be the duty of the government. And since petro-dollar was abundant at the time, the administration of General Gowon did not find it particularly difficult turning this sentiment into reality.

What was however lacking at that time, was the unwillingness of government to answer the practical question of critics, which was whether the government was in a position to fund education sufficiently for all times. The controversy and rancor generated by the take-over are yet to subside completely throughout the country. By 1980, some of the state governments were almost choking from the financial weight of education. As a way out, some of them initiated processes that would lead to the handling back of these schools to their former owners. That process of tactical disengagement was yet to be completed before another military government took over power in 1983.

A prominent religious leader, Archbishop Olubunmi Okogie, went to court over the issue, during the second Republic. He observed "that Private schools have always been better managed than public schools in the country. And when private and public schools co-exist, there is always a healthy rivalry". According to him, the government needs to build its own schools to discourage the so-called private educational enterprise.

The Universal Primary Education in Nigeria

In 1976, General Olusegun Obasanjo (rtd) started off the apparently ill pre-pared Universal Primary Education (UPE) scheme. The scheme, along with others, suffer from ill-preparation and inadequate statistics. For example, while it was envisaged that some eight million pupils would enroll for the scheme, the figure ballooned to twelve million. The situation was also compounded by shortage of infrastructure and personnel.

The scheme was hinged on the strong financial position arising from a buoyant world oil market. The Federal Government undertook the finance of teacher education, so as to produce sufficient manpower for the implementa-tion of the scheme. New teacher training colleges were constructed, and the existing ones were expanded, while all education students in tertiary institu-tions were taught, fed and housed free. They were even paid allowances for books and upkeep. All of these were aimed at sustaining the scheme. Expectedly, the enrollment in Teacher Training Colleges expanded manifold. Within a year of the implementation, there was an increase of about 74 percent in teacher enrolment. By 1980–1981 academic session, the Federal government washed its hands off teacher education, because it was financially strapped. Instead of the scheme yielding good dividend, the reverse became the case. Shortly afterwards, the state governments started closing colleges of education, retrenching and retiring teachers, and placing embargo on appointments. These actions were taken at a time when teachers were greatly needed for the increasing enrolment of students. According to the Guardian publication of January 29, 1987, "the country needed 190,000 teachers in secondary schools". The problem arose because of the state government's inability to finance the Education Bill.

There was return to the course of free primary and secondary school educa-tion by the five states won by the Unity Party of Nigeria (UPN), in the 1979 election. The after effect of the mass education embarked upon by the former Unity Party of Nigeria (UPN) in the controlled states was the woeful performance of these states in the 1985 West African School Certificate Examinations.

The New National Policy of Education 1981 tagged (6-3-3-4) was embarked upon in 1981. It provides for six years of primary education, six of secondary education, the first three years being considered the Junior Secondary School (JSS) segment, and the last three, the Senior Secondary School (SSS). The Junior Secondary School provides courses that are both pre-vocational and academic. The three years of Senior Secondary School are meant for those willing, capable, and able to have a complete six years of Secondary Education. It is these products that are to proceed to the University for the four years degree course. The scheme was beset with problems, and the first of such problems was inadequate publicity. While the new scheme is generally acknowledged to be better than its predecessor, because of the relevant vocational skills that it would impact on pupils, the implementation was however, hampered by lack of infrastructure, and the right caliber of teachers.

The most critical problem however, is the haphazard manner with which various states of the Federation are implementing the program. The Onabamiro committee, which planned the implementation, recommended that the scheme should start in 1976, so as to have the first set of the Junior Secondary Students (JSS) in 1982, and the Senior Secondary School students SSS in 1985. The political turbulence of the second Republic did not allow the program to start as scheduled. Only a few states like Kaduna, and the Federal Government Secondary Schools started the scheme in 1982. While states like Oyo, started in 1985, and some others later. But even for the few states where the scheme has taken off proper, there are enormous problems. The case of Kaduna State, which started earlier since 1982 is instructive. Although, the first set of students admitted under the new policy sat for their Junior Secondary School final examination, they were unable to proceed to the fourth form, because the vocational centers where the graduands would have gone, to improve their skills, were just being set up. The delay in the take-off of vocational centers has been attributed to the delay in the acquisition of equipment. The problem that confronted the early implementation of the program also confronted the others as well. In Oyo state, only very few centers had adequate equipment for use. Many had been under construction since the implementation started, while the buildings of some are yet to be erected. Those graduands that would have gone to improve their skills in vocational skills in the proposed vocational schools, were sent back to their parents. While those that are willing, and able to have a complete six years of secondary education proceed to the forth year, that is, the first year of the Senior Secondary segment (SSS) of the education structure.

The classrooms are so crammed that many students sit on the window sills. Also, students have to provide desks and chairs for themselves. The problems were succinctly summed up by an educationist, Mrs. Aguwu, in 1987,"while some schools have no laboratory and workshops, others have these structures, but no equipment. It is only when a nation realizes that education is the best defense of a nation, that it can be serious about its educational/annual Budget allocation to education. Education receives one of the lowest budgetary alloca-tion in Nigeria, whereas the military (defense) allocation is always the highest.

Logically, the crisis is carried over to the other sectors of the education hier-archy, the secondary and the tertiary segments, since the policy at the federal level is passed on to the state and local government levels. The introduction of the Universal Basic Education (UBE) by the past regime of President Olusegun Obasanjo in 1999, is a step in the right direction. But again, the implementa-tion is fraught with a lot of problems. Some states in the federation are taking the policy more seriously than others. The continued flux and instability in the system has eventually resulted in the introduction of yet another policy in the educational system of the country. This time, it tagged the 9-2-3 system of edu-cation, in which case, the pupils will be expected to stay in school compulsorily for nine years, after which they can decide to further their education to the senior secondary level, and later to the tertiary level. Ostensibly, the first nine years are meant to have equipped them for one vocation or the other, with the aim of making them vocationally equipped, to be on their own. One can only be optimistic that the objective will be achieved, given the antecedents.

CHAPTER EIGHT

CHILD NEGLECT

DR S.V. KOBIOWU

INTRODUCTION

The institution of marriage brings two consenting adults together, for the purpose of producing children in all societies. When the children start coming, it is necessary for the parents to take care of them, from the helpless state in which they come into the world, till they will be in a position to fend for themselves. The act of taking care of children is very cumbersome, and entails the use of foresight. Since babies cannot talk, parents are in a situation of guessing what they want at a particular point in time. All children require that their basic needs are met. How these are met, what values adult place on children, the amount of discipline administered, and how responsibilities are given—all these aspects of child-care are managed differently in different communities.

Many years back the parent-child relationship was very fragile, children were seen as miniature adults, and character training was the dominant concern. These days, children are no longer seen from adult point of view only, fundamental changes, which are currently affecting the society, are also affecting child-care norms. Child-care experts are no longer dogmatic, when giving advice. Parents are encouraged to understand each child, and to trust and relate their own feeling to that of the child. Physically handicapped and mentally retarded children often require a great deal of attention, compared to normal ones.

According to experts in child-care studies, the first social learning or the child occurs in the home. His earliest experience with his family, particularly with the mother, are important in determining his attitude towards others, as well as the expectations they have of other individuals. The mother gratifies the child's primary needs for food, for alleviation of pain, and for warmth. As time goes on, the mother's presence becomes associated with the satisfaction of needs. She is seen as the source of pleasure, contentment, and relief of tension.

As such, the child soon learns to search for, and reach out to his mother, whenever he/she is hungry, in pain or uncomfortable. If the mother is nurturant, or gratifies the child's needs promptly, and effectively, the child will develop favorable social attitudes. The child will not hesitate to approach other people whenever the need arises, and will respond to others in a friendly manner.

In a nutshell, the child's interactions with the mother form the basis for his/her reactions towards others, (Lindsay 1971). The interaction between a child and the mother lays the groundwork for the child's development of a sense of trust, or distrust in later life. Rewarding, and gratifying experiences with the mother makes the child to trust her, and by implications, others. In contrast, a mother who is not dependable, or does not attend to the child's needs satisfactorily, produces a sense of distrust of herself, and by implication, of others in later life.

Millions of children are growing up under economic, social and psychological conditions, which hinder their optimum development. Their problems are pointers to the fact that something is wrong with their pattern of interaction, their parents, or the neighborhood in which they live.

Child Neglect Across Cultures

According to conservative estimates, in New-York city (1976), one out of every four babies born is associated with a pattern of continued neglect. Many children experience other forms of substitute care, like guardianship, fostering, or even adoption, in place of parental care. The substitutes for parental care, shift responsibilities for the child, and deny the opportunity for an on-going personal relationship with his/her parent or the guardian. Some parents are immature, and overwhelmed with the new, or over-demanding responsibilities. While others are poorly equipped with knowledge needed to give care to children, and maintain family balance.

The consequence of these, is gross child neglect. Many children run away from their homes, and migrate to cities, to live among others, like themselves. Some do this as a way of escaping from inadequate care, or for lack of care from parents, and guardians. While others engage in such in an attempt o seek for independence, individuality, or adventure, by moving away from what appears to them a rather hostile environment. This situation drives many teenagers to delinquency, and this is further compounded by the inadequate treatment, and shoddy rehabilitative resources available.

Delinquency has both cultural and legal basis, and may be viewed as the existence of conflict between the norms of society, and conduct of an individual, (Duseck, 1970). Some cases of delinquency may reflect in improper socialization, or may be due to child neglect, while others could be induced by environmental circumstances.

The vast majority of delinquents come from poor families, living in deteriorating or economically deprived neighborhoods, usually adjacent to the center of a city, (Downes and Rock, (1963). However, not all impoverished children living in slums actually become delinquents. It is therefore obvious that socio economic factors are not the only significant antecedents of delinquency. Personal insecurities, neglect, and psychological problems, stemming from disturbed family relationships, may also be inherent in the delinquent's background.

In all societies, the act of reproduction is carried out to ensure the perpetuation of mankind. The passage from childhood to adulthood is one accompanied by the process of socialization, and parents are responsible for effecting this process. Socialization as a process involves inculcating the norms and values of the society into the young ones, coupled with taking care of them socially, morally, and financially among others.

Socialization is therefore part and parcel of child-care. However, some parents fail in this task. As a result of this, such children suffer neglect in one form or the other. Children that are neglected go through a kind of socio-psychological trauma, and have problems fitting well into the society in later life. As a result of the unfavorable circumstances that avail themselves to the neglected child, he or she develops a sense of insecurity.

Such children, on attaining teenage status, may start to deviate from the culture of the society. Teenagers who deviate from the culture are referred to delinquents. Delinquency could therefore be seen as a social terminology, denoting law breaking, particularly by persons not considered as adults. Acts engaged in by delinquents are considered as immoral, or as anti-social. Such include fighting, stealing, robbery, drug addiction, drug trafficking, and among others. He thus becomes a terror to the society. He is useless to himself, his parents and the society at large.

According to a popular philosopher, education is the vehicle by which a meaningful development is attained. As a result of this, the case of the uneducated child described above, can only hinder development, it can never promote it.

In conclusion, it is also a well-known fact that a child from a broken home will perform poorly at school. Since the child's parents are not living together, he/she will most likely be inadequately catered for. The consequence of divorce, among others, is that the child either lives with one of his parents, or he is transferred to a relative who doubtlessly denies him enough attention, if any at all. There is usually nobody to motivate the child, when necessary. He feels neglected. For this reason, an otherwise naturally gifted or talented child may have his talents truncated. Feeling of neglect and insecurity lead to the child's weak academic performance, as he is treated as an outcast by the society. In combating delinquency therefore, the attempt should be one, which aims at alleviating or reducing the incidence of child neglect, rather than focusing on other possible causes of delinquency.

CHAPTER NINE

CORRUPTION IN NIGERIA

DR E. O. OLOYEDE; DR S.V. KOBIOWU AND DR I.O. ARANSI

Outline

1. What is corruption?
2. What are the manifestations?
3. What are the causes?
4. What are the consequences?
5. What are the likely solutions?

INTRODUCTION

The term corruption is defined by the Oxford Advanced Learner's dictionary of current English as an immoral act, especially the offering and accepting of bribes. Although the term corruption can be defined in different ways, for the purpose of this exercise, it is defined as a situation in which gratification is demanded, or offered and accepted, before performing official duties, which otherwise should not have attracted any gratification. In the same vein, it also means the gratification demanded or offered and received, to pervert the course of justice. The problem of corruption has assumed a dangerous dimension in recent time, so much that it is generally believed that if something drastic is not done it may lead to the total collapse of the morality of the nation.

Prevalence of Corruption

In Nigeria, as elsewhere, corruption manifests itself in every aspect of the public service. For a long time, it has been felt by the generality of the Nigerian citizenry for example, that most police officers are corrupt, we all felt very helpless. However there have been instances when the corrupt practices in the police force were carried to an embarrassing and ridiculous extent. Policemen extort money from transporters, commuters and passers-by openly, and routinely, without due regard for the laws they are paid to enforce. They erect illegal check points, demand for particulars they are not interested in checking, and even when they meet a motorist with correct documents, they will still proceed to collect bribe. All these happen because the so-called ogre, known as corruption, has become for many, a way of life, and it is the order of the day in the country. It is common knowledge that policemen buy their way to check points and similar duties at a heavy cost to them, and they are expected to make regular returns to their superior officers, or face re-posting.

In the government ministries, it is quite clear that where a minister or a director general in charge of a ministry, has received some gratification in abuse of his office, he can hardly be expected to effect discipline within that ministry. Similarly, a judge who is corrupt can hardly be expected to make a report of any corrupt magistrate, neither can he be expected to give a fair and unbiased judgement.

It is not that official corruption descended on us after independence. Indeed, the phenomenon of official corruption developed with political administration, not only here, but virtually everywhere, in varying degrees. Sufficient legislation were made against corruption in our criminal code, however most of the sections dealing with official corruption in the code have fallen into disuse, due to reason best known to the authorities. The truth is that we are now living more or less in a lawless society.

One is apt to adduce reasons for the prevalent high level of official corruption in Nigeria. In the first instance where the leadership is corrupt, the followers should not be expected to do otherwise, since most of our elders, be it in military or civilian, have either by their action or inaction encouraged corruption in Nigeria, as in many other parts of the world.

Efforts at Stemming Corruption in Nigeria

With the exception of the short-lived Muritala Mohammed regime, and the frantic effort made by the Buhari/Idiagbon administration to address the issues of official corruption in Nigeria, other administrations at the center have greatly contributed to the problem, by openly indulging in various corrupt practices, and until recently when the present government took it upon itself to fight this cankerworm.

In a society where accountability and probity are not treasured by both the public office holders and the polity at large, such a society is bound to be a very corrupt one. In Nigeria, we do not accord accountability and probity, a priority in our scheme of things. Nobody feels concerned about any public officer who lives above his or her means. In fact, most Nigerians consider top government appointments as the easiest avenue to make money, and people expected such appointees to be very rich by the end of his/her tenure.

Our culture, which gives unnecessary recognition to the wealthy ones, irrespective of the sources of the wealth, does not help the situation. It is only in Nigeria that a known treasury looter is given chieftaincy title, in as much as he doles out some amount of money to the traditional ruler. We worship wealth, not minding the sources of such wealth, and in an attempt to acquire wealth, which ultimately leads to recognition in the society, public officers among others, indulge in various corrupt practices.

There is equally the factor of our value system, which has changed over the years. In the past, good name was cherished and treasured. Most people would not want to do anything that could tarnish the family name, and whoever does it, was regarded as a 'bastard' and an outcast, no matter how rich within the family. However, nowadays, the emphasis has shifted to money, and most people are now sacrificing their good names for money, knowing fully well that their dented image can always be redeemed by their wealth.

The judiciary has also not been spared in the problem of official corruption in Nigeria. The judiciary everywhere is supposed to be the conscience of the nation, and is supposed to be manned by people of high integrity, who are incorruptible. However, it is not surprising that since the level of official corruption has risen so high, and so deep-rooted, only a fool will permit himself to be charged to court, or if charged to court to be convicted since 'settlement' is possible at any stage. And since the 'offer' of settlement is, in most cases, irresistible to the 'offeree'.

A public officer who is charged with receiving one hundred million Naira as 'kick back', or with defrauding the government of the same amount, can be sure never to appear in a court or convicted, if he is willing to 'spend' only a quarter of it to 'settle' the police, or/and the judicial officer(s) concerned.

The economic problem currently facing the nation, which in itself was an offspring of massive corruption and gross mismanagement of the national economy, has aggravated the problem of corruption in Nigeria. Attempts to make ends meet, or to maintain a basic living standard have forced many public officers who would not have been involved in corrupt practices into it. With the current rate of inflation in Nigeria, hardly can any public officer live a 'decent' life with his/her legitimate monthly income. The situation has degenerated to a point where every salary earner has to look elsewhere to supplement his/her income, and in such circumstances, one is easily lured into corrupt practices, at least to be able to cope with the 'hard times'.

Consequences of Corruption

The consequences of official corruption in Nigeria cannot be over-emphasized. In a situation where everybody sees appointment to a public office as a money making venture, rather than a call to serve one's 'country, with all honesty and sincerity of purpose, the future of the country is seemingly not bright except there is a sudden turn around. It should be realized that if the problem is not seriously addressed, and with the present lukewarm attitude to it, succeeding generations will always introduce sophistication into it.

With official corruption everywhere, we are gradually eroding confidence in our public institutions, and once all confidence is lost, especially in our judicial system, anarchy takes over. The effect of anarchy may be too severe for us to bear.

Within the past decade, Nigeria has witnessed unprecedented corrupt practices, especially at official levels, in which corruption was elevated to the level of state policy. However, hope is not lost, if and only if Nigerians, especially the people at the helms of affairs, are decisively ready to tackle the problem. As Dr. Akinola Aguda puts it, "the present administration needs to make a clean break with the past, as a deliberate policy, of eliminating corruption and indiscipline in the nation's body politic". He further observed that "unbridled corruption and indiscipline had considerably weakened the nation, and the only way out of it is for present administration to severe links, if any, with the nation's economic cabal, and also make a clean break with the past".

Speaking on corruption and indiscipline as the evil we must fight in Nigeria, a former head of state, Major General Muhamadu Buhari (retired) observed that there was no way the country's resources would be adequately mobilized without tackling the problem of corruption and indiscipline.

To reduce the problem of official corruption to the barest minimum in Nigeria, those at the helms of affairs should lead by examples. They should be ready to give full account of their stewardship, and should be ready to defend their earnings.

The general populace should equally change their attitude toward accountability. Every public officer should be keenly watched, and whoever misuses his or her office in any manner, should not for any reason be spared, so as to serve as deterrent to others.

The present administration is striving somewhat frantically, to remedy the situation, by establishing a number of agencies that are charged with the duty of checking official corruption. Such agencies include the Economic and Financial Crime Commission (EFCC), Independent Corrupt Practices Commission (ICPC), and the National Agency for Food Administration and Drug Control (NAFDAC), among others.

Unnecessary emphasis should no longer be placed on money. Money should not be seen as an end in itself, but as a means to an end. Our emphasis should be honesty, in both public and private life, and people who display honesty in any form should be highly regarded, in order to encourage others. Any public officer who misuses his/her official position should not only be punished, but should be seen to have been punished, by all and sundry.

Above all, eliminating corruption, or at least reducing corruption to the barest minimum in Nigeria, requires the collective effort of all Nigerians, and the earlier we do this the better for the country.

CHAPTER TEN

THE SCOURGE OF AIDS

DR S. V. KOBIOWU

INTRODUCTION

Acquired Immune Deficiency Syndrome (AIDS) is caused by retrovirus. Internationally, it has been agreed the virus be called the Human Immunodeficiency Virus (HIV). The virus transmits through infected body fluids. The semen containing HIV would not cause infection of a woman if the walls of the vaginal or cervix are unbroken, or unscratched, or unbruised. But if however it is in contact with breaks in the vaginal wall at ordinary intercourse, AIDS can be transmitted.

Similarly, split at the anus interior at anal intercourse can allow infections. This means that those at high risk of being infected are homosexual, bisexual, men (both swingers), promiscuous men that frequent prostitutes, partners of these men, and drug addicts, who share needless. The immune system protects the body against infections. A part of the system is a series of defensive blood cells. Some of B-cells produce infection-fighting compounds called anti-bodies. Others are called T-Cells. T-Cells assist the B-Cells to fight infection (in form of anti-bodies) suppressor. T-Cells stop the productions of anti-bodies by B-Cell. In healthy people, there are 2 helpers to T-Cells. AIDS damage them. According to researchers, AIDS cannot be contacted through casual contact, like hugging or kissing, and hardly through oral sex (tonguing and sucking). No one knows why the people with HIV eventually develop AIDS, but the potential for cross-species transmission is now clear. It has been said to have found its way to West Africa sub-region, through the European soldiers, who ravaged Africa, after the 1st World War.

The question one may like to ask at this juncture is; Does it mean that social changes hastened in a way, the spread of HIV? Yes! Starting from the 1960s, war, tourism, and commercial trucking, forced the outside world on Africans, as at the time drought and industrialization prompted mass immigrations from the countryside into the newly teeming cities. As a French medical historian—Marko Grmek notes in his book <u>HISTORY OF AIDS</u>, urbanization shattered social structures that had long constrained sexual behavior. Prostitution exploded, and venereal diseases flourished tremendously. Hypodermic needless came into wide use during the same period, creating another mode of infection, worldwide. More that 12 million people are presently infected with HIV. The great majority live in Africa, South of the Sahara.

In laboratory tests, researchers from the U.S. center for diseases control found the HIV-2 was associated with AIDS. In the same vein, going by what we have seen so far, we have to say that HIV-1 causes AIDS in 90 percent of those infected, while HIV-2 causes AIDS in 10 percent or less, according to Harvard, an AIDS control specialist. Apparently, anyone infected with HIV-2 will progress to AIDS after 4 or 5 years, but that's still in the realm of reduced virulence.

An Egyptian horologist named Ewald, categorically puts it, "it is no surprising that HIV Virus which eventually cause AIDS have slow transmission in areas with low sexual contact, and HIV-1 far more rapid transmission in areas with high sexual behaviors.

Edward and a few other researchers the view that AIDS cannot be contacted with sexual immorality. In laboratory tests, some researchers at the university of Alabama found that Senegalese HIV-2 didn't even kill white cells when allowed to infect them in a test tube. Yet HIV-2 is a killer in the more urban and less tradition bound Ivory Coast. In a survey of hospital patients in 1967 at the city of Abidjan; researchers from the U.S. Centers for disease control found that HIV-1 was in fact very deadly.

In a nutshell, these disparities suggest that HIV assume different personalities in different settings, becoming more aggressive when it's traveling rapidly through a thickly populated area. But because so many factors affect the health of infected people, the strength of the connection is unclear.

This is exactly the right way to think about virulence, concluded virologist Stephen Morse of New York's Rockefeller University. He remarked that a pathogen like HIV has a wide range of potential, but we can't say what pressures are needed to generate a particular outcome. The best answer to Morse's question may come from laboratory studies. A handful of biologists are busy devising series of tests and experiments to see in one or more ways, precisely how transmission rates of HIV could be minimized, if not totally eradicated in Africa as a whole, and Nigeria in particular.

Since experts on AIDS control have been working day and night to know the source of the virus, Medical teams of different socio-economic, and political backgrounds, keep on launching world-wide campaigns to guide against varying indiscriminate sexual behavior.

In Egypt for instance, research shows that people are dying in highest magnitude of AIDS. Enlightenment campaign gave an estimate of 2 out of every 10 Egyptians (if we go by Egyptians hypothesis), are contacting the dreaded virus. The same is true in Malawi Republic, whose commonest social problem is AIDS.

Even countries like Tanzania, Zimbabwe, Mozambique, Botswana and Zambia i.e. those that shared boundaries with Malawi have similar AIDS problem. Though not quite rampant in Nigeria, but research from a handful of biologists, medical scientists, Zoologists, and virologists, to mention but a few, show that AIDS virus is rapidly growing among Nigerians.

CONTRIBUTORY FACTORS TO THE SPREAD OF AIDS

It is pertinent to examine some of the contributory factors. One of the major factors had been traced to the danger from tourism, which constitutes about one third (1/3) of the continent's largest proportion of AIDS carriers. Tourists from other countries mainly Europe, Britain, Spain, Canada, China and India and some other continents, are the major carriers of AIDS virus. Some of them, after contacting our women folks during intercourse, pass the virus on to other able bodies. Such people eventually become victims of AIDS.

Another factor could be traced to the cultural norms. The cultural norm associated with sexually transmitted diseases is circumcision. Circumcision rites in most African communities, for example Nigeria, Ghana, and Gambia to mention but a few, are carried out in such bizarre fashions.

Perhaps, cultural norms attached to circumcision gave them the belief, that circumcision of children must be done in groups. Even some parts of Nigerian still belief in such practice till today. Their young children are circumcised in groups of ten, fifteen and in twenties, with only one razor blade, and in hideouts. As soon as a child is circumcised, they merely clean up the razor blade (without sterilization) and then go to the next child, until they finish for a group of more than three, four and five children. The similar phenomenon is the case of using one syringe to inject more than two, three, four or five children.

One syringe according to the medical direction is meant for not more than one patient at a time, but the reverse is that case in many hospitals, clinic and other health institutions.

Other related occurrence is the issue of blood transfusion. In most hospitals, clinics and other private and public maternity centers, blood is not properly screened before being administered to the patients.

The unscreened blood always poses danger to the health of the patients: they might have been infected with AIDS virus, and once transmitted to a healthy patient, such person automatically becomes an AIDS carrier.

Another factor could be the problem of child abuse. A cross section of young girls in our primary and secondary schools drop out from school, due to early pregnancies. Incidents where girls of about 12 years, or even less, are impregnated by adults, are common, and some of these youngsters fall victim due to the depressed economic situation in the country. Many young ladies are compelled to fall in love with tourists, who have few dollars to play around with. Unless something is done to reduce or discourage the rate of drop-out from schools, the country will continue to loose the active young ones, who have taken to prostitution as a way of achieving their ends, with the risk of contracting the disease.

CAN HIV BE TAMED AND COMPLETELY ELIMINATED

Until recently, medical science seemed well on its way to controlling the microbal world: Series of case studies by researchers on AIDS prevention claimed that there may not be a drug or vaccine on earth that could subdue such a protean parasite. But from a Darwinian perspective, killing HIV is not the only way to combat AIDS.

We know the virus changes rapidly in response to outside pressures. Logic suggests that if we simply apply the right pressures within a community, or even within a patient's body, we may begin to tame it. It is well known that condoms and clean needles can save lives, by preventing HIV infection. From an evolutionary perspective, there is every reason to think they could do. In a 1991 study, researchers at the National Institute of Health (NIH) calculated the rate at which people are infected. Safer sex precaution reduces the rate at which people contacted AIDS virus, according to this study.

In the meantime, more than 12 million people are carrying HIV today, and those who have acquired full-blown AIDS, are dying at an alarming rate. In order to reduce the death rate, a cross section of Public Health Officers at the University of Toronto Canada in 1991 introduced the use of condom.

Their worldwide campaign on sex devices focused on the use of condom, and cheap medicine. If these devices are widely used, aids infections can reduce drastically, all over the world.

WHAT ARE THE SYMPTOMS OF AIDS?

AIDS becomes indicated when the person has a fever, sweat at right, and usually has swollen glands in the neck, the armpits and the groin. He or she looses weight, has diarrhea, looses his appetite, and feels tired. These symptoms are usually found in other viral infections, but if all these symptoms persist for more than three weeks it is necessary that such person should consult a doctor immediately. The medical teams on AIDS have even proved that most carriers of the virus remain perfectly healthy. Between 15 and 30% will go on to more severe forms of AIDS in a 2 to 5 years period.

REMEDIES AND METHODS TO BE ADOPTED TO ELIMINATE AIDS IN OUR COMMUNITIES

In the first place, government and individuals should make it compulsory to wage serious war to discourage prostitution. Greater number of drop-outs from schools join the wagon when there is no other means of livelihood, and they must survive. Jobless parents rely wholly on their young girls for the family's daily survival (bread). These are the girls who work and operate in hotels and restaurants, sometimes as prostitutes. Government must assist in providing job opportunities, to discourage temptations from our girls looking for hard currencies from the sugar daddies who exploit the girls sexually.

Similarly, frantic efforts must be made to encourage one child, one blade method, for children and infants' circumcision. Societal norms and culture that ignore this should be totally eradicated. To reduce the rate, at which the AIDS virus is spreading, the use of condoms must be widely encouraged.

Further, in order to combat its spread, efforts should be made to organize periodic seminars for both primary and secondary school teachers, pupils, and university lecturers, including the public transport drivers, who should also be educated, to ensure that everyone is acquainted with what AIDS is, and how it can be prevented. People should also be made to understand the fact that presently, there is no known cure for AIDS and its virus yet.

Various countries should endeavor to discourage the activities of the so-called prostitutes. This activity should be authoritatively declared illegal by the existing regimes, in different societies, so that those engaging in the deal may find other means of livelihood, other than prostitution.

The most baffling situation is that the prostitutes know that AIDS exist, and have strong belief that there is no known cure for it, but still keeps indulging in unprotected sex, even without the slightest form of precaution.

Furthermore, various international organizations had been giving series of enlightenment campaigns, as to the danger of AIDS/; the United Nations Children Fund (UNICEF) Non-Governmental Organizations (NGOs), MALAWI Media AIDS Society (MASO), Zimbabwe's National Aid Policy, and each country's ministry of health, have all declared a full-scale war against the incurable virus. What is left is to strictly adhere to the series of campaigns against the no cure disease "AIDS".

Since there is no treatment for AIDS presently, one can only offer supportive therapy in form of: Blocking the entry of the virus to the cell, through vaccine and reception blocker. Blocking replication of the virus, through block viral protein synthesis, and improving the immune cell function through marrow transplant. The campaigns that governments are mounting to prevent the spread of AIDS by sexual routes must be backed up by a campaign by professionals, to prevent the smaller but potentially equally hazardous spread of AIDS, at the handling of the body fluids level, by promptly attending to people who have the disease. Sufferers of AIDS virus should consult qualified medical personnel for effective diagnosis and prompt treatment.

Improperly treated condition gives way to the organisms proliferating, and becoming very disastrous to health. Unless the affected person is treated during the early stage, the disease will continue to grow, and eventually affecting the brain, thus causing mental problems and insanity, among other ailments.

CHAPTER ELEVEN

UNEMPLOYMENT IN NIGERIA

DR S.V. KOBIOWU

INTRODUCTION

Unemployment is a condition whereby a factor of production (especially labor) is not demanded in the labor market. Unemployment is a situation where the supply of labor is greater than the demand for labor at the prevailing wages. An unemployed person can be defined as a person who is willing to work at a wage rate currently being paid to other individuals who possess similar qualifications and experience with him, but cannot find any job. Unemployment is a condition that is undesirable, for it means wasted human resources.

There are social as well as economic arguments against unemployment. However, if there is full employment, the economy will be unable to work flexibly and efficiently. Expanding industries will find it difficult to attract the additional labor they require.

There are three distinct but related dimensions to the unemployment problem.
1. Many people are frustrated by lack of employment opportunities; they include both those without work, and those who have jobs but want to work longer hours or more intensively.
2. A large fraction of the labor force, both urban and rural, lack a source of income both reliable and adequate for the basic needs of themselves and their dependants.

3. A considerable volume of unutilized or under-utilized labor forms a potential productive resource, which ought to be brought into use.

CAUSES: From various studies, (Nwazuoke, 2004; Cassen, 2004; and Newsam, 2004), among others, it is revealed that many things have been responsible for unemployment, some of which are discussed below.

a. **Population:** The population is growing at a faster rate than economic growth. For example the number of school certificate holders and graduates provided every year is greater than the number of available job openings.

b. **Lack of Labor Mobility:** In most cases, labor is not mobile, while some have insufficient supply.

c. **Use of Machinery:** In modern times, producers prefer the use of labor saving machinery, to employing more hands, and as a result, less people are employed.

d. **Changes in Foreign Exchange Earnings:** When there is a deficit in foreign exchange earnings, the government usually places an embargo on employment.

e. **Closure of Industries:** (Poor funding or no raw materials). This has caused a lot of people to be thrown out of wage (employment).

f. **Lack of Information:** Lack of adequate information on job opportunities can be a cause of unemployment, especially that of the frictional type.

g. **Educational Planning:** The demand for labor would fall, if there is excessive rise in wage rates. Such a rise can encourage employers to substitute capital for labor. Trade union pressures may be the cause of excessive wage increase.

h. **Lack of Creative Exploits:** The issue of creativity as a condition for mastering the environment has become necessary, because it would appear as Rogers, quoted in Nwazuoke (1997) seems to be saying, that unless individuals, groups and nations can imagine, construct and creatively devise new ways of relating to societies' complex changes, 'the lights will go out'

Having analyzed the various causes of unemployment, irrespective of the nation and her economy, one will quickly want to analyze the various types of unemployment that we have, before critically relating the studies above to Nigeria's situation in particular.

Types of unemployment. There are various types of unemployment.

a. **Cyclical Unemployment:** This is the most serious type of unemployment. It is characterized by various differences in demand. It goes to the extent that it affects all the sectors of the economy, thereby causing mass unemployment. Reconciliation of full employment and stable prices becomes difficult in this situation because, in spite of high level of unemployment, the rate of inflation is high.

b. **Seasonal Unemployment:** In some occupations, like building and agriculture, there is demand for labor only at certain periods of the year. For instance, demand for bricklayers is usually high during the dry season.

c. **Frictional Unemployment:** In the course of inventions and innovations, productive factors may be switched from one occupation to another. This transfer occurs when factors become unemployed and the demand for them falls because the demand for their services in the present occupation has fallen, though the factor may be demanded for in the other occupations. Most technical undertakings aim at innovations, which may lead to a fall in demand for labor in industry. This will lead to unemployment. For example, the invention of automatic loom reduced the demand for hand weavers in the textile industry.

d. **Residual Unemployment:** A situation where the handicapped cannot be gainfully employed. A physically and mentally handicapped finds it difficult to get jobs.

e. **Regional Unemployment:** When the basic industry of an area declines without any increment, then the workers affected become unemployed.

f. **Technological Unemployment:** This arises as a result of changes in the techniques of production, when a technique of production is invented, less number of workers may be needed to do the same type of work than before. Those retrenched as a result are said to suffer from technological unemployment.

Why is unemployment a problem in Nigeria?

Having analyzed the concept above, it will be more relevant and appropriate to see Nigeria as a case study.

When the trainees, or apprentices are trained, the needed capital to establish becomes a problem, which invariably affects them, rendering them more or less as 'educated—illiterates'. Secondly, more government policies are ill-motivated, or misdirected, as a result of national loyalty to state, or local government allegiance. Some policies often tend to favor some group and de-favor others. Rather than being objective, unnecessary sectionalism of tribal sentiments are introduced.

Another problem relative to Nigeria's situation is leadership problem. Most leaders of many Nigerian governments have not approached the unemployment problem with the seriousness that it deserves, which has resulted in engaging in anti-social menace, by those unemployed, breeding such as armed robbery, burglars, swindlers (419), etc. Another problem is the get-rich quick syndrome by the youths, who are able-bodied, and fairly educated, but who refuse to engage in legitimate jobs, that have prestige and dignity.

CHAPTER TWELVE

THE MENACE OF DRUG ABUSE

DR S.V. KOBIOWU

INTRODUCTION

The World Health Organization (WHO) 1964, defined drug as any substance that is capable of modifying one or more functions or structures of an organism when ingested. The word, substance, has been preferred, to the word, drug, in current psychological literature, owing to the fact that there are certain substances which cannot be categorized as drugs, but which nevertheless do alter the functions and structures of an organism, when ingested. That is why the associated disorders are called substance use disorders.

In view of the fact that the substances are so many and different from one another, emphasis is most often placed on narrow brand of substances called 'psychoactive drugs'. These are the drugs, which particularly affect the mental functioning and psychological make up of the individual users. As a result of this emphasis, the term 'drug use' and 'drug abuse' will be employed in most of the discussion.

According to the Nigeria Food and/Drug Act, 1974, "A drug is any substance, or mixture, manufactured, sold, or advertised for the purpose of diagnosing, treating, mitigating, or restoring, correcting or modifying organic functions in man. Substance dependent behavior develops through a number of stages. The stages are:

SUBSTANCE USE

This is the first stage, when the individual first uses a particular substance or drug. The drug may be used either as a result of it being prescribed for the treatment of a specific ailment, or as a result of peer pressure, or out of sheer curiosity. In most cases, drug use is a voluntary act.

DRUG MISUSE

This is the use of drug for other purposes, than those which they were prescribed e.g. codeine tablet for abortion, instead of its use for curing headache. Heroine is usually prescribed to subdue severe pain, but later users use it for other purposes that are physically satisfying to them.

CRAVING

It is a periodic and intense desire to use a particular substance, or drug. The desire is usually so strong that in most cases it sounds as a psychological drive or motivator.

While it is not everyone who uses drugs that becomes addicted, many people do, Mayo 2006).

TOLERANCE

It is a condition in which larger doses of a drug are increasingly needed over a long period of time, in order to produce the same effects that the smaller doses of the drug produced at an earlier stage of using the drug. Tolerance is a physiological attempt by the body to adapt to, and neutralize the effect of the drug.

PSYCHOLOGICAL DEPENDENCE

This is the condition that used to be called "drug habituation". It is a condition in which drug users feel that he or she cannot function adequately without using a particular drug. In most cases the individual adjusts his or her social life to suit the requirement for the use of the drug e.g. stealing, burglary, theft, etc.

Nature has tried very hard to protect the brain, and messing around with drugs can change the way the brain works naturally. When one takes drugs, some parts of the brain starts to disagree on what to do, and that creates a big problem. The brain can solve problems, be creative, be logical, make plans, and do almost anything else one can think of. All parts of the brain work together, to keep us healthy, intelligent, and happy, (Drug Enforcement Administration, 2006).

PHYSIOLOGICAL DEPENDENCE

This is the condition that used to be called "drug addiction". It is a condition in which a drug user is both emotionally and physiologically attached to a particular drug, to such an extent that the individual cannot function adequately without using the drug. The condition results from the prolonged use of certain drugs, which makes the drug incorporate to the body system.

In the absence of the drug, the system reacts as if it were deficient or incomplete. Drug users suffer therefore from serious physiological consequences, if the particular drug is not available for use.

WITHDRAWAL SYNDROME

It is also called "Abstinence syndrome". It is a cluster of signs and symptoms, which a drug abuser suffers from, when the drug to which he is physiologically dependent is either not available for use, or is suddenly prevented, or withdrawn from his use.

The characteristics of the condition include anxiety, nervousness, muscular cramps, increased heart-beat, dry mouth, profuse sweating, tremor, shaking of the hand, and the generalized feeling of ill health. Other symptoms are headache, diarrhea, running nose, dizziness and fainting; sneezing, general discomfort, and hallucination, among others. In extreme cases, death results (e.g. drugs such as heroine and morphine).

The effects of drugs depend on which class they belong. Generally, psychoactive drugs are divided into 8 or 9, compressed to 3 groups, which are:
    (i)   Depressants
    (ii) Stimulants
    (iii) Hallucinogens

DEPRESSANTS

These are the types of drugs, which slow the activities of the body, reduces the responsiveness of the body, lower the attention span and induce sleep. Some classes of depressants are:

1. ALCOHOL   e.g. beer, spirits, wines, 'ogogoro';
2. NARCOTICS   e.g. Opium, Morphine, Heroine;
3. BARBITURATES   (sleeping pills) e.g. Phenobarbitone, Armylobabitone;
4. TRANQUILIZERS   e.g. Librium, Valium, (anti anxiety drug) Mandrax.

ALCOHOL

Specifically, the long-term effects of alcohol include delirium.

A condition characterized by delusions, perceptual delusions, and visual hallucination, especially at night. The individual also suffers from tremor of the extremities, disorientation, and acute fear. Alcoholics often suffer from a condition known as KORSAKOV SYNDROME, which is characterized by memory deficiencies for a recent event, and the tendency to confabulate. In all cases most depressant drugs produce euphoria and tolerance, for the drug develop rapidly. Most of the drug also produces physiological dependence. Consequently, abusers of dependants suffer from withdrawal syndrome.

STIMULANTS

These are drugs, which increase the activities of the body. They promote mental alertness, increase wakefulness, and increase the social desires of the users. The drugs also produce a feeling of euphoria, and make the users to be more energetic and outgoing. Large doses of stimulants induce confusion, heart palpitation, nervousness and insomnia (sleeplessness).

The following are common categories of stimulants:

A. AMPHETAMINES   (Sleepless tablets) e.g. Benzedrine Dextroamphetamine, Pre ludin, Ritalin, Prophus.
B. COCAINE
C. NICOTINE in tobacco products.
D. CAFEINE in coffee, tea, kolanuts.

The specific pharmacology effects of some stimulants are as follows:

Large doses of amphetamines induce Psychosis. The intake of cocaine often precipitates a type of skin disease known as COCAINE DERMATITIS. In both forms of Psychosis, the individual often manifests hallucinations, flight of ideas, and delusions of grandeur. Stimulants do not generally produce physical dependence. There is therefore no withdrawal syndrome associated with the non-availability of the drugs. However, stimulants produce very strong psychological dependence, especially the use of tobacco products.

HALLUCINOGENS

They are also called Psychedelic drugs, because they produce radical consequence on the mind, by altering the users state of consciousness. The drugs induce vivid imagery, distortion of awareness, and distorted perception. They also induce feelings of euphoria and depersonalization. Decreases in the span of attention, and increase in heart beat, and body temperature, are often reported by users.

Some common categories of hallucinogens are:

- A. CANNABIS (Marijuana) whose active ingredient is Delta-9-Trans-Tetrahydrocannabinol (T.H.C.).
- B. L.S.D. (Lysergic acid diethylamide). The most pointed and devastating stimulants.
- C. PSILOCYBIN from a Mexican mushroom.
- D. MESCALINE from peyote cactus.

Some of the specific effects of members of the hallucinogens are as follows:

Cannabis makes the eyeball to be bloodshot and red, and at the same time induces blurred vision, poor estimation of time, and over-confidence. In some situation, it makes users to have dry mouth, and have a voracious appetite. Lysergic acid diethylamide induces paranoid, indecision, and lack of concentration. Users may report having colors and seeing sounds, a condition known as SYCATHENIA: Day dreaming, disorientation of time, place and person, and frequent episode of depersonalization, are also associated with the use of cleaning fluid, nail varnish and synthetic substances such as PCP (angel dust) and MTD. Their pharmacological effects are a cross between effects of stimulants and hallucinogens. There is no physical dependence associated with the use of hallucinogens. There is no physical dependence associated with the use of hallucinogens, and most of these other drugs. Consequently, there is no withdrawal symptom associated with their unavailability for use. However, a synthetic variety of cocaine known as CRACK induces physical dependence, and the usual withdrawal syndromes, when the drug is not available for use.

INHALANTS

There is another drug or substance that can be abused, that is if it is not used as prescribed or directed, by the producer. Examples of these inhalants are Aerosols and gasoline. It can also be found in glues, solvents, butinitrate (room odorizers). It is usually in gas or liquid form, and it can be inhaled or sniffed by the users of these drugs. The effect of these drugs on the abusers and reflex control, heart failure, and sudden death, if the abuser did not stop misusing it in a wrong way.

Adolescents and youths of between ages 15–30 years constitute the high-risk groups, with females getting more involved than they used to. Other groups of abusers are the so-called young executives, prostitutes, drivers, conductors, graduate civil servants, artistes, etc. Some reasons have been put forward for drug abuse, these are as follows:

1. Social pathologies, such as unemployment, and parental deprivation.
2. Emotional and psychological stresses, such as anxiety, frustration and economic depression. Peer group pressure, characterized by the desire to be accepted among friends, or in social circles.
3. Peer group pressure, characterized by the desire to be accepted among friends, or in social circles.
4. The desire to achieve success in a competitive world.
5. Warped materialistic value system in the society, such as crave to get rich quick.

Signs of drug use and drug paraphernalia, and possession of drug related paraphernalia, such as pipes, rolling papers, small decongestant bottles, possession of drugs, peculiar plants, seeds, or leaves is ashtrays, or clothing pockets, odor of drugs, smell of incense of other "cover up" scents. Identification with drug culture, like drug-related magazines, slogans on clothing, and hostility in discussing drugs.

EFFECT OF DRUG ON ABUSERS

The effects of drug on the abusers are many. The effects are as follow:

There are memory lapses, short attention span, difficulty in concentration, poor physical co-ordination, and slurred or incoherent speech, indifference to hygiene, bloodshot eye, and dilated pupils, among others.

There are changes in behavior, like distinct downward performance in school, or work place, increase absenteeism or tardiness, chronic dishonesty, lying, cheating, stealing, trouble with the police, changes of friends, evasive in talking about new ones, increasing and inappropriate anger, hostility, irritability, secretiveness, reduced motivation, energy, self-discipline and self esteem.

The physical, psychological, social and economic consequences of the drug problems are becoming more obvious and disturbing.

Examples are as follows:

Physical consequences: are Brain damage, liver damage, hypertension, excessive heart beat, chronic bleeding, damage to unborn babies, and also (Acquired Immune Deficiency Syndrome).

Psychological Consequences: are sleeplessness, anxiety, depression, psychosis, craving desire, withdrawal symptoms and premature death.

Social Consequences: are loss of job, family disintegration, expulsion from school, delinquency, criminal offences, stealing, assassination/murder, rape, armed robbery, destitution, prostitution, and premature death.

Socially, Hydes (1968) described drug abuse as the use of chemical agent to the point where it seriously interfered with economic, social or health functioning. According to Omoluabi (1993) drug abuse is the excessive use of a substance, either for a longer period of time than it was prescribed, or in doses, which are over and above those that were prescribed. The adverse consequences of drug abuse include anti-social behavior, particularly on health. It ruins characters, and career. Drug abuse can be avoided by the abuser, by not taking drug without the doctor's prescription, and desisting from the attitude of 'try and see'. Parents should devote some of their time to the training of the children, morally, and religiously. The government also should provide work for the unemployed people, and make effort to rehabilitate drug victims.

CHAPTER THIRTEEN

ARMED ROBBERY AS A SOCIAL MALADY

DR S.V. KOBIOWU

INTRODUCTION

Armed robbery is one of the social vices, which has for quite a long time, become a cankerworm, and has eaten deep into the fabric of the society. This has been as a result of some social delinquencies. Mainly, in Nigeria today, as elsewhere, people found in this notorious act, are people in their early twenty, to about thirty years of age, both male and female. A number of factors have contributed to the alarming rate of armed robbery in Nigeria, as in other places, as they affect the state of the nation. Among the factors are:

1. Unemployment;
2. High urge for acquiring wealth;
3. Extravagant spending'
4. Unequal distribution of resources and income;
5. Lack of compulsory/free education to the University level;
6. Inadequate provision of social amenities for members of the public;
7. High cost of living;
8. High inflationary rate; and
9. Economic recession.

1. **Mass Unemployment:** The rate of unemployment in the past two decades has increased by almost two hundred percent. This has been the result of increase in the number of graduates from tertiary insti-

tutions, compared to the low level of employment opportunities available for these graduates. It is obvious and inevitable that an idle hand is a veritable instrument for the devil. These people also want to live like their counterparts who are gainfully employed. And since they could not get a job, and in a bid to earn their living, they are tempted to engage in armed robbery, and such other fraudulent acts.

2. **High Urge for Acquiring Wealth:** Many contemporary youths are always thinking and aiming at acquiring wealth, by any means, like their older counterparts. They are not concerned about what effort these elderly people had made, and the stressful period they had passed through, but for the mere fact that they see them living comfortably, and using big cars, they also want to live similar life-style, at all cost, including armed robbery.

3. **Extravagant Spending:** Ostentatious display of wealth by the minority in our society has influenced negatively most of our youth, to the extent that they feel the urge to acquire money by all means, including armed robbery.

4. **Unequal Distribution of Resources and Income:** Many people have been pushed to indulge in this criminal act (armed robbery) as a result of inferiority complex among their contemporaries in the society. A wide gap in the distribution of income has made some people in the society not to have adequate purchasing power like others. It is only the people with high income that can boast of being able to afford some basic social necessities, while people with low income can hardly have their three-square meals daily. But in an attempt to do this, they may force themselves into unruly acts, such as drug trafficking and eventually armed robbery, so as to get quick money, with which to meet up with the standard of their kin in the high-income group.

5. **Lack of Compulsory/Free Education to the University Level for all children:** This situation has made accessibility to higher education virtually impossible for children of poor parents. Some of the people engaging in armed robbery are very brilliant and highly intelligent, but because they have no access to formal education, they divert into another area and become delinquents.

6. **High Cost of Living:** It is no exaggeration that the cost of living in this country has gone beyond the reach of the common people. Most people are ready to lay their hands on any available means of getting

their daily bread, at least to keep the body and soul together, including of course armed robbery.

7. **High Inflationary Rate:** For over a decade now, the rate of inflation has risen rather astronomically, thus, increasing arbitrarily the
prices of essential commodities in our markets. However, there had
not been a commensurate increase in the salaries and wages of the
workers. Consequently, one can imagine the hardship experienced
by the workers, not to talk of the unemployed people. If the workers who are employed are crying as such, what is expected of those
who are not employed, and who have no means of getting their living; undoubtedly, unruly acts, and actions are imminent, including
armed robbery.

8. **Economic Recession:** This is the product of political upheaval and
impasse that have befallen the country since about ten years ago.
Economic recession has also given birth to high inflationary rate,
and high cost of living. Assuming that there is political instability,
there might not have been this recession in the economy, and may be
the cost of living might have been within the reach of the suffering
masses.

9. **Non-Challant Attitude of the Federal Government to Education:**
Since October 1979, when the then General Obasanjo handed over
power to Alhaji Sheu Shagari, the second Republic President, the
attitude of the Federal Government of Nigeria toward the education sector has not been encouraging. The Nigerian Universities had
suffered so many industrial actions from their staffers. There was a
time when a whole academic session was cancelled, due to industrial
actions by the Academic Staff Union of Universities (ASUU). Had it
been that the Federal Government has been more interested in education, it should have provided the necessary fund, and equip all the
Universities with equipments necessary for the smooth running of
the institutions. This lack luster attitude has made many students to
abandon schools, and join various gangs of men of the underworld,
including armed robbery gangs.

From all the above, it is clearly shown that the government has a lot to do
in reducing or curbing the rate of armed robbery in our society. Among the
possible solutions aimed at curbing the alarming rate of armed robbery, the
following appear imperative:

1. Reducing unemployment, by creating more employment opportunities. If job opportunity is created or provided for the graduating

students of various levels of education, this will reduce, if not totally eradicate, the number of people who are willing to work but could not get employment. And an idle hand is the 'devil's weapon'.

2. Extravagant spending and high urge for wealth accumulation should be checked by the government. The Federal Government should use all the available weapons within its reach to reduce, ostentatious consumption.

3. Compulsory Education up to the University level: The Federal Government should enforce compulsory and free education to every Nigerian child up to the University level. And any child who is less intellectually endowed should be trained in vocational courses, and placed in the relevant sector of the economy.

4. Inadequate provision of social amenities to the public: it is obvious that it is only the state capitals and the Federal capital that have the required social amenities. And this should not be. Every part of the country should be provided with adequate social infrastructures, so that every citizen will have access to social infrastructures, as this will not allow or give room for one person to covet other people's properties.

Above all, the non-challant attitude of the people at the helm of affairs in the country towards education must change for the better, if this country is to have a brighter future for the generation yet unborn. The care-free attitude towards the welfare of the students and the teachers at the various educational levels should be discarded, for the better.

CHAPTER FOURTEEN

ALCOHOLISM AS A SOCIAL MENACE

DR S. V. KOBIOWU

INTRODUCTION

Alcoholism is a chronic illness, characterized by the habitual drinking of alcoholic beverages, to the extent that the health and social functioning of those involved, are impaired. Alcohol, when consumed in excessive amount, is habit-forming, and the alcoholic can neither restrict himself from drinking, nor control the amount he consumes. He is both physically and psychologically dependent on alcohol.

In the United States, alcoholism may be viewed as a disease, a drug addiction, and a symptom to a physical disorder.

An alcoholic is a person who drinks and has problems from drinking, but goes on drinking, anyway. The committee of the World Health Organization has defined alcoholics as "excessive drinkers, whose dependence upon alcohol has attained such a degree, that it results in noticeable mental disturbance, or in an interference with their smooth social, and economic functioning, or who show the preliminary sign of such development.

It is hard to say just what personality traits lead to alcoholism. The potential alcoholic usually has a feeling of isolation, low tolerance for frustration, tendency to act impulsively, a sense of rebellion and a low capacity of perseverance. He develops his addiction gradually.

In the early stages, he may drink only for social purposes, and at the same time enjoys the tension-lessening effects of the drinking. In the next quarter, he begins drinking alone, and soon to hide his growing addiction, and this leads to drinking in secret. At the final stage, he becomes a chronic alcoholic, when he considers it necessary to indulge habitually on morning drinking, to be able to face the on coming day.

There are two types of alcoholic: the steady drinker, and the periodic alcoholic. The steady drinker consumes large quantities of alcoholic. He does not only drink daily, but goes on excessive drinking.

People drink alcohol in three main kinds of beverages.

1. **Beers:**—This is made from grain, through brewing and fermentation, and it contains from 3%-8% alcohol.
2. **Wines:**—This is fermented from fruits, such as grapes, and contains 8%-12% alcohol.
3. **Distilled Beverages (Spirits):**—Under this are Whiskey, Gin and Vodka, which averagely contain 45%-50% alcohol. Drinkers may become addicted to any of these beverages.

TYPES OF ALCOHOLISM

There are four main types of alcoholism.

1. **Alpha Alcoholics:** They have a psychological dependence upon alcohol, they are apt to behave badly when drinking, and create problems for themselves, but they are able to control their drinking, and can stop when they want to.
2. **Beta Alcoholics:** These people develop physical symptoms, such as gastritis and cirrhosis of the liver, but they may not be either psychologically or physically dependent on alcohol.
3. **Gamma Alcoholics:** Are psychologically and physically dependent on alcohol. They are addicted to it, and cannot control their use of it.
4. **Delta Alcoholics:** They resemble gamma alcoholics, except that they may often be relatively light drinkers; their difficulty is that they cannot abstain from drinking for even a day or two, without experiencing tremors or hallucinations.

Alcoholism can be found among successful business-men, artists, scientist, skilled workers, homeless vagrants, and criminals, students, unemployed people, etc. It is also a growing problem among women and teenagers.

PHYSICAL AND MENTAL EFFECTS

Alcohol is easily absorbed from the digestive tract into the blood stream, and is quickly distributed throughout the body. It affects nearly all the cells, especially the brain. It acts as a depressant, and not as a stimulant. As alcohol concentrates in the blood, more and more centers in the brain are affected.

The amount and type of food in the stomach affects the absorption rate. Drinking when the stomach is filled is less intoxicating than when it is empty. The food in the stomach, which contains fat and protein, delay alcohol absorption. Body weight is also a factor. The heavier the person, the slower the absorption of alcohol. The damaging effects of alcohol may be greatly exacerbated, if the drinker is also using drugs. The combination of alcohol and sleeping pills has sometimes been fatal, even when both were taken in non-lethal doses.

At the same time if one takes too much of alcohol, the centers controlling the heartbeat and breathing are depressed, and it leads to death.

After a prolonged period of drinking, lasting from a few hours to several days, the alcoholic is usually dehydrated and in need of food. He also needs medication, to settle his inflamed stomach. As he emerges from the drinking episode, he may suffer nausea, headache, thirst, weakness, etc. These symptoms can be accompanied by convulsion, and tendency to become easily injured or infected.

Chronic alcoholics always develop a number of physical traits and disorders. Such as redness of the eyes, puffiness of the face, skin diseases, liver disease, etc.

He also suffers from mental disorders, hallucinations, impairment of memory, etc.

Drugs such as tranquilizers, antibiotics, aspirins, and even cold remedies, have been found to interact dangerously with alcohol.

SOCIAL ASPECT: Alcoholism is one of the most expensive diseases, in terms of money, and happiness. Socially, alcoholics involve not only themselves negatively but also their friends and relatives. Their disruptive influence often results in broken homes, divorces, burden-someness, welfare, fatal traffic accident, and suicide, among others. Industry bears a grave burden with the alcoholic, who not only looses time from his own job, but who is also a serious accident hazard to the other people working around him.

DRINKING AND YOUTH

Patterns in drinking vary from community to community, and the patterns among young people seem distinctly affected by prevailing social customs and cultural influences. More girls than boys abstain from drinking. Religious influence or affiliation is often a significant factor in abstention.

At the college level, drinking is commonly a group activity, often meant to satisfy social needs. This leads to automobile accidents, sexual misconduct, and aggressive behavior, that can easily lead to lasting physical damage.

Students who drink heavily, and who persist beyond college age, may have this as an inherited character trait from heavy drinking parents. Now, they have a desire to drink as a means of reducing anxiety. Or to them, it may appear as a sense of rebellion in general, and they may prefer to spend their leisure time drinking, rather than participating in normal social activities.

Also, a person's reaction to a situation is sometimes influenced by the reaction he or she anticipates. For example, if a young non-drinker expects to get drunk from one bottle of beer, he/she is likely to act intoxicated, even though he/she is not. By contrast, heavy drinkers take pride in the amount of liquor they can ingest. At parties, they may seem to drink without adverse effects, because they know how to compensate for those effects. Aware that they cannot walk well, they will not try to walk or will take care not to stagger.

DRINKING AND DRIVING

Alcohol impairs a driver's judgment, and performance, and as a result, the alcoholic driver is a significant cause of traffic accidents, particularly those causing serious injury and death. In some areas, more than half the fatal accidents involve drivers who have been drinking heavily.

To help law enforcement agencies determine whether a driver has been drinking, many chemical tests have been devised, to determine the presence of alcohol in the body. Alcohol concentration can be measured in the breath, saliva, the blood, or in the urine.

TREATMENT

The treatment of alcoholism can be considered in the following stages: emergency, and long term care.

The most effect treatment of alcoholism includes both medical and psychiatric measures. For more serious alcoholics, psychiatric hospitalization for a period of time is the best. It provides opportunities for medical care, and social rehabilitation.

Complete abstinence from alcohol is an essential part of the treatment, and the alcoholic, like the drug addict, experiences a number of unpleasant withdrawal symptoms. Very often, he needs sedatives during this period.

CHAPTER FIFTEEN

POVERTY AS A SOCIAL PROBLEM AND THE ROLE OF EDUCATION IN THE SOCIETY

DR S.V. KOBIOWU: DR.(MRS.) Y.A. AJIBADE:
AND DR E.O. OLOYEDE

INTRODUCTION

Poverty is essentially a relative concept, a condition measurable only in terms of the living standard and resources of anyone in society, at a particular time.

Individuals are poor when they are significantly deprived, relative to the circumstances of their fellow human beings. As Galbraith (1958) observed, people are poverty stricken when their incomes, even if adequate for survival, fall markedly below those of other members of the community, that they cannot have what the larger community members regard as the necessary minimum for decency. They are degraded, for, in the literal sense, they live outside the grades or categories which the community regards as acceptable.

United Nations Development Program (UNDP,1997) understands poverty primarily as with-holding from the poor, the opportunity and ability to choose to lead a life of human dignity. For those affected, this means a short life, a lack of knowledge, and political and social marginalization, among other things.

What is necessary for a decent standard of living is a matter of social definition, which may change over time, but the fact remains however, that the poor are not simply at the bottom of the stratification hierarchy, but are almost, in a sense outside the margins of that hierarchy. They form what some have called an "under class" in the stratification system.

Poverty could also be taken to be a standard of living that is below a particular minimum standard. The official definition that was adopted by National Assistance Benefits (1966) was "the level of resources at which one becomes entitled to supplementary benefits". Aboyade (1984) defined the Nigeria poor as paupers, beggars, disabled, with no visible means of sustained livelihood, the single unemployed, the homeless vagrant families, and the social deviants who subsist precariously on the edge of the society.

One may then regard or recognize the poor as either one not willing to provide for himself and his family, or may not be able to because of sickness, disability, or constraints, demanding presence in the home or temporarily without job, because there are no jobs available at a time, and place for someone with his talents or skills. It may also be due to lack of skills to get a job, or skills for a job that does not provide an adequate income to meet the economic needs, because the monthly wage is too low, the hours of work available are insufficient, or a combination of the two.

Many studies revealed that a consistent and significant section of the population is living in poverty stricken circumstances at one time or the other, to say nothing of many others who, at certain crucial periods of their life (e.g. the old families with young children) may temporarily lapse into poverty. Such studies indicate clearly and forcefully that poverty is still very much with us, and that any complacency about rising standards of living in Third World countries as inevitably banishing poverty, must be quickly dismissed. Those most vulnerable to poverty at the present time are the old, the sick, disabled, the unemployed, and insecurely employed, low wage earner, the large family, and single parent (usually fatherless) family.

With the introduction and definitions of poverty, one can see that it is not only an individual problem, but also a social and national one, which poses serious threat to the peaceful existence and development of the society. A large proportion of the deviant behavior in the society, such as crime, immorality, divorce, alcoholism, drug abuse, and other delinquency acts have often been attributed to poverty. There is also the general belief that eradication of poverty in the society will reduce the incidence and severity of these social ills.

TYPES OF POVERTY

Identified are two main types:
1. Primary poverty, which is also known as underserved or involuntary poverty. This arises when the income of an individual or family is insufficient to provide for the basic needs required for physical efficiency.
2. Secondary poverty, also known as deserving or voluntary poverty which arises from the mismanagement of an income that would otherwise have been sufficient for the satisfaction of basic human needs.

CAUSES OF POVERTY

Causes of poverty may be divided into three categories namely:
(i)   Societal or structural factors.
(ii) Natural or circumstantial factors.
(iii) Individual, attitudinal and behavior factors.

(i) Social factors refer to external factors, not caused by the victims, such as class stratification, unemployment or level of employment, level of technological development, and insufficient income. Also included are such issues as government policies, social, political and economic factors, as well as many dependants, and over-population of a state.

CLASS STRATIFICATION: This is the category or position one falls into, particularly as regards one's career in the society. It is discovered that the higher the level of class stratification, the lower the level of poverty. The converse is also applicable. One would see that doctors are in a high class, compared to clerical officers. Many people are poor because they fall into lower levels in the class stratification hierarchy.

UNEMPLOYMENT: This is a situation in which one is not able to secure a job, and is not earning anything. Majority of the people are poverty stricken, due to this problem of employment. Many degree holders are unemployed, while many with vocational training are unable to acquire money to invest on their business. Hence, many are poor.

LEVEL OF TECHNOLOGICAL DEVELOPMENT: High level of technological development, which creates a situation whereby machines produce faster and cheaper than man, may lead to unemployment. On the other side, low level of

technological development may cause low production, which may make prices
of things go up, and one's income could become insufficient to meet the basic
needs. Consequently, poverty occurs. Also, higher demands on advanced skills
may lead to some being pushed out of jobs or not being employed.

INSUFFICIENT INCOME: This also affects badly the Third World nations. It
is a condition whereby the income is not sufficient to cater for ones basic needs,
which leads to poverty.

GOVERNMENT POLICIES: This also dictates the level of the standard of living of the people in the society. Poor leadership will eventually bring economic
recession, which makes the nation's currency to be devalued. Arising from
this, could be over-dependence on foreign materials and huge investment on
external debt servicing, instead of investing on agricultural produce and other
social utilities. All these bring inflation and increase the level of poverty in the
society.

POLITICAL INSTABILITY: This also drives away investors, causes inflation,
and reduces the standard of living. It may also be possible that one is gainfully
employed, with enough income, but if there are too many dependants from the
family and friends, it may make one poor. One Yoruba proverb puts it that "a
rich man among six poor men is equal to seven poor men".

OVERPOPULATION: A society is overpopulated when the people in the
society are more than the resources needed to cater for them. This also causes
poverty.

(ii) Natural or circumstantial factors may make one unproductive or not fit for
employment. For example, the sudden death of the bread-winner, especially the
father, which may affect the children; bad luck and disasters, such as accidents.
Others include blindness, fire destroying one's properties, mental retardation,
amputating hands or legs, lameness, deafness and dumbness, and other natural
disasters, which usually lead to poverty.

(iii) Individual, attitudinal and behavior factors, which include lack of education, large/polygamous family, spending meager income on useless and
unnecessary materials. Others include alcoholism, pools betting, gambling,
immorality, wasteful spending, inability to plan for one's future, uninformed

career choice, lack of initiatives and skills, laziness and pride, lack of ambition, goals or life plans.

LACK OF EDUCATION: Education is a branch of the knowledge industry. It is the whole experience of living, which may either be formal or traditional. Formal education is the type given at a particular place with stated curricula, age grades, and time, with the aim of supporting the discovery of new knowledge to create job opportunities for people. Formal education also provides specific skills that will determine one's qualifications for various careers and also provide abilities and energies for a professional work or service.

Traditional education is received at home and from members of the society, in preparation for the world of work. Vocational training like carpentry, hunting, farming and others, are inculcated into an individual, which make him to be self and gainfully employed.

Members of poor families, often, can hardly afford to continue their education beyond secondary school. The greater the degree of poverty, the more limited educational opportunities become. So, with the passage of time, the limited educational opportunities available to the poor serve to perpetuate and accentuate the inadequacy in income and wealth. Education is also the chief means by which the lower class individual may improve his social position. Due to poor standard of education and government's non-challant attitude to educational development, many people do not get the basic education, and hence, are not loosened from the bond of poverty. Though it is true that a man with little educational background can still rise to a position of power and wealth by hard work, or perhaps by stealing, cheating and luck. Today, not only do most of the jobs available demand more in the way of specialized training, the size and bureaucratization of many business and industrial organizations make it more difficult for the individual who lacks, at least the minimum educational qualifications, to make his mark in the society.

LARGE FAMILY: As over-overpopulation of a state causes poverty, also many people are poor due to family over population. The number of nuclear and extended family members they are financing is more than they can cope with.

Many people with many wives and children cannot afford to provide for the basic needs of the entire family members. A large number of children constitute more drains on available resources, and may impoverish the family, by reducing the spendable income of the family.

Spending meager income on useless and unnecessary materials could also result in poverty. Contrary to the reasonable expectation that the poverty of the poor would make them more austere and prudent in expenditure and life style, one discovers that their life style is at times characterized by lavish behaviors, such as poor financial management, extravagance and wasteful spending which are barriers to upward mobility and success. The usual outcome of this is borrowing and abject poverty.

OTHERS: Alcoholism, pools betting, gambling, immorality, and conspicuous living habits hamper the life chances of individuals and social units because of material deprivation. These make one to be disengaged from major social institutions of the society, and eventually result in strong feelings of helplessness, dependency and inferiority, with lack of impulse control.

EFFECTS OF POVERTY: Poverty as a social problem is loaded with many negative effects.
* Many social vices like armed robbery, rape, child abuse, alcoholism and others, have been attributed to poor standard of living of the populace, due to poverty.
* Moreover, poverty limits the life chances of individuals, and social units, because of material deprivation.
* The poor is also usually disengaged from major social institutions of the society, and there is absence of prolonged and protected childhood.
* Frequent cases of abandonment of wives, children and siblings, due to inability to provide for them is another effect of poverty.
* There is little ability to plan for the future, which brings about resignation to fate.
* Many illnesses, tension, and frequent quarrels, are negative effects produced by poverty.

ALLEVIATING POVERTY IN THE SOCIETY:

The problems mentioned here form only a fraction of the very many factors that cause poverty. Suggestions made here could affect even those problems not listed. It is believed that to every problem, there is a solution. However, no amount of suggestions can totally eliminate poverty in human society. Nevertheless, the following should help to reduce and alleviate poverty in one way or the other.

One of the United Nation Millennium Development Goals (MDGs), which was adopted in September 2000 at the Millennium Summit, is to eradicate extreme poverty and hunger. One of the three main areas identified by

Association for the Development of Education in Africa (2002) in achieving these goals is investing "adequate resources in human development, namely education.

Education is one of the major instruments to be used for the alleviation of poverty. Education supports the development of the arts, and thus offers a contribution to the aesthetic environment and also contributes to our rate of economic growth, as well as a person's economic productivity. Income tends to increase with educational levels, and through education one could rise to a higher level and higher class, and thus alleviate poverty. Through education, the "eyes will be opened", and people would learn ways of making a better living, either through government or self-employment. Education helps to develop greater awareness of, and ability to participate effectively in the democratic processes, which in turn helps to alleviate poverty.

Mention here must be made of the necessity to provide education that will promote gender equally and empower both male and female who both have roles to play in the development of the society.

CHAPTER SIXTEEN

RELIGIOUS INTOLERANCE

DR S. V. KOBIOWU

INTRODUCTION

Religion is one of those mysterious phenomena that permeate into the life of all human kind. Every society, be it civilized or uncivilized, has some kind of religion. In civilized societies, religion is properly structured, with laid down procedures, which are properly and carefully written down in books. Individuals do accept, or reject the belief system. In some societies, there could be only one religion, to which everybody belongs, or must accept. In which case, the individual is not free to belong to any religion of his choice, but must belong to a particular one, either by virtue of birth, acquired position, knowledge and wealth.

However, in less civilized societies, the belief system is not always well-structured and organized, with laid down procedure. In other words, every individual or group here has his own god, and worships it in his own way.

Religion, fundamentally, is the cultural premise of the belief system of a people. This can lead to certain practices of worship rituals, propitiation and offerings of all kinds.

Religion is the strongest element that can exert the strongest influence upon the thinking and living of people. In other words, every society, be it civilized or primitive, has some kind of religion.

The various forms of religion in the world today are as follows:

(a) Traditional religion;
(b) Hinduism;
(c) Buddhism;
(d) Confucianism;
(e) Taosim;
(f) Judaism;
(g) Christianity;
(h) Islam;

(a) **Traditional religion:** This is sometimes known as primitive religion, for it is being practiced by the less civilized societies, like the Red Indians of India, and some African societies. This type of religion has no specific founder, and the year it was founded remains debatable.

(b) **Hinduism:** Hinduism is the religion practiced in India for many years. It is claimed to have been founded about 13th Century B.C. in India. The founder is also not known.

(c) **Buddhism:** It is also a religion founded in India by Gantama Budha, during the 6th century B.C. Its teachings are different from those of Hinduism.

(d) **Confucianism:** It was founded in the 6th century B.C. in China. The founder is K'ung clim. His followers called him K'ung Futzu. This was later Latinized as Confucius.

(e) **Taosim:** The 6th century B.C. was no doubt a century of religion founding. This was founded by Laotze, in China.

(f) **Judaism:** It was founded in Palestine by Abraham, during the 2oth century B.C. It is the religion of the Jews.

(g) **Christianity:** Founded in the 1st century A.D. by Jesus Christ. The religion has spread all over the world. It is claimed to be next to communism in population.

(h) **Islam:** It was founded during the 7th century A.D. by Mohammed. It is also spreading fast.

(i) Other world known religious in the world include: **Sikrs Jaina, and Perseas**. All religions in the world believe in the existence of a super natural being, known by various names. Similarly, all religions teach discipline, character training and love. It is nearly impossible to get all the people in the world to believe in one religion.

CONCEPT OF RELIGIOUS INTOLERANCE

Religion has been described as a cultural premise of belief system of a people. The belief system can make individuals differ essentially in personality and other character traits. Some are bound to be more committed to their belief and practice than others. That is, some individuals could be weak, and fall short, in the practices of their religion. Others, who think they are strong in the faith, by obeying the rules of the religious game, naturally feel offended by the religious behavior of the weaker ones. This could lead to religious intolerance, even within the members of the same religion. For this reason, it is common to hear about ex-communications, expulsion, ban, or restrictions, on some members of a religious group, and so on.

In many cases, such individuals or groups who have been ex-communicated, expelled or restricted from the practice of their religion, do feel aggrieved, and form or organize their own religious practices slightly different from their original religion. This can easily create and cause some disaffection among the members of the group. In a number of cases, such split can bring about open confrontation between the two contending groups. Religious intolerance, therefore, means the inability of some people, be they individuals, or groups, to tolerate the weak, or deviant behavior of other members. It may also mean the inability of members of one religious group to tolerate the practices of another religious group. Such intolerance can easily breed tension, and discord, and may result in open confrontation.

CAUSES OF RELIGIOUS INTOLERANCE

In the introductory aspect, the meaning of religious intolerance, as the inability to bear or tolerate the behavior, the weakness or the religious practice of another person or group, was discussed. By this definition it is apparent that religious intolerance could be inter-religion or intra-religion. In other words, religious intolerance could be found amongst members of the same religion, or amongst members of different religions. Little wonder that in Nigeria, there are many factions known as 'sects' within the Christian faith. There is the Catholic Church, which is said to be the original Christian Church. But because of some kind of religious intolerance, the Protestant church broke away from the Catholic Church. For similar reasons, there are many denominations within the Protestant church. Similarly, there are factions in Islam. In Nigeria, two very strong factions are known to exist in Islam—Darika and Izale factions. As has been mentioned earlier, intolerance, within the same religion is known as intra-religious intolerance, while intolerance between different religious is known as inter-religious intolerance. As we have already noted, both types exist in Nigeria. Here you can find the obvious and possible causes of religious intolerance in our society. These include:

(a) **Weak and deviant behavior:** The weak and deviant behavior or some individuals within the same religious group could cause other members to be angry. This could easily result in disaffection and disintegration of the group. For instance, if the religion demands that all members must refrain from taking alcohol, other members must have cause to be angry with such an individual who indulges in such, and this could be a source of religious intolerance.

(b) **Powerful Leaders:** Some religious leaders sometimes become so powerful, that they do not want other followers to question their activities. When this happens, members who could not tolerate such powerful behaviors could campaign against such leaders, and or break away from such a religious group, and establish their own independent religious groups, or join another religious group.

(c) **Desire to win more members:** Every religious group, be it primitive, or civilized, wants to win more membership for its religious group. This can very often bring about disaffection and confrontation. This could be very dangerous to the existence of the society, and like any other form of intolerance should be avoided. Religion is a matter of personal conviction, and no amount of force can make others good followers of the religion.

(d) **Feeling of Superiority:** Some people, out of ignorance, feel that they are a superior group, and so, their religion. They look down on other religious groups, and would like to impose their religious faith on the others. This is so because every human group feels superior in its own right, and any attempt to despise their existence and belief is resisted most vehemently.

For a group of people that occupy an entity to live as a united nation, with one destiny, they must learn not only to tolerate the religions of all the other groups that exist in the country, but must also respect them, and their ways of life.

CHAPTER SEVENTEEN

THE EFFECTIVE TEACHER: A REVIEW

ONI, C.S. PH.D

<u>Who is an Effective Teacher?</u>

Either in the Pre-primary, Primary, Secondary or Tertiary institution, an effective teacher is some one who is competent to executive his/her school assignments and responsibilities adequately. Precisely, an effective teacher according to Miller and Rose (1975) is one who can demonstrate in the classroom and on the job as a builder of bridges between expanding and changing subject matter on one side and a wide range of personalities on the other. Such personalities include those who are willing to learn new concepts, new attitude and new skills.

The effective teacher is one who enables the students to learn what they need to know at the right time, rapidly and well. An effective teacher possesses some qualities and techniques, which contribute significantly to his/her effectiveness. A few of the qualities of an effective teacher listed by Miller and Rose (1975:2) are:

1.   Competence in the subject being taught;
2.   Mastery of the techniques of teaching;
3.   Resourcefulness and creativeness;
4.   Knowledge and application of evaluation procedures;
5.   The desire to teach; and
6.   Ability to develop good personal relationships

Each of the qualities listed are briefly reviewed as follows:

COMPETENCE IN THE SUBJECT BEING TAUGHT

The statement is sometimes made that a person who knows how to teach can teach anything. It would also be more accurate to say that, in some instances, a competent teacher can learn new subject matter in a shorter time than an inexperienced subject matter specialist. Whichever way one looks at this statement, there is no substitute for experience.

A competent teacher will do a better job of staying one lesson ahead of the class and will be more at ease with students than an inexperienced teacher. In fact, it is advisable not to attempt teaching a subject which a teacher lacks knowledge of and experience in. The teacher should be thoroughly competent in the skills to be taught as well as in the related information in whatever subject in thecae specializes.

MASTERY OF THE TECHNIQUES OF TEACHING

Tibbetts, J; Akeson, M. and Silverman, M. (19968:79) discussed the importance of the application of good techniques of teaching students in the classroom. The authors reviewed some of the teaching techniques, which the competent teacher should employ as follows:

1. Prepare each lesson to be sure that the best use is made of the students' time;
2. Plan the lesson and relate everything that happens in the learning situation to the objective of the lesson; and
3. Ensure that the planning is flexible enough to capitalize on special interest or special experiences of the individual student in the class.

In conjunction with the listed techniques, Miller and Rose (1975:4) discussed some of the techniques required by the competent teacher in presenting lesson to students in the classroom as:

1. speak
2. organize instruction according to students learning capacities;
3. repeat and emphasize key materials in such a way that it stands the best chance of being remembered;
4. conduct a demonstration skill fully, and
5. provide practice sessions and performance tests in such a way as to promote and develop desirable skills and attitude.

The above review on teaching techniques is a pointer to the fact that, no matter how competent a teacher could be, he must possess a great deal of knowledge and know about the ways through which students learn. The teacher should also be proficient enough to provide opportunities for students to learn and be able to understand the complex skills of teaching.

RESOURCEFULNESS AND CREATIVENESS

Only the incompetent or lazy teacher uses the same method or technique all the time. The methods that work well for one individual, one class or one lesson may not necessarily be satisfactory in another situation.

In this regard therefore, a good, competent teacher should be alert to detect confusion, misunderstanding, or lack of interest among students, and be able to adjust his or her approach instantly to correct any difficulty.

Miler and Rose 91975) emphasized two main reasons for varying instructional procedures with different classes or individuals as:

i.   Individuals differ to a marked degree in native capacity.
ii. Individuals differ in background, experience, and in learning pattern.

Taking a critical look into the two reasons above, one will observe that the learning pattern or style of individuals differ from one to the another. Thus, the rate with which a particular individual learns a particular subject depends to a large extent on how well he adapts his learning pattern to the method through which the teacher presents the material. Precisely, what we are saying here is, the teacher-student relationship should work both ways. The teacher must be quick enough to modify instructional procedures so that learning will be facilitated.

Resourcefulness is also demonstrated when the teacher designs a new instructional aid to help illustrate a principle and uses the current event to emphasize a concept. He also can build an advanced project to develop his own competence in whatever subject he teaches.

KNOWLEDGE AND APPLICATION OF EVALUATION PROCEDURES

A competent teacher is like a good cook who keeps testing the food to see if the flavor is right, or like the craftsman who uses the senses of sight, smell, and touch to indicate when the power tool is cutting properly and safely.

A competent teacher must be sensitive to the ways the students are learning. This can be done periodically by examinations if the questions are designed to find out whether or not the students have achieved the objectives specified for instruction. In other words, can the students demonstrate the level of skill, knowledge and attitudes for which the instructional program was designed?

Thorndike (2000:33) highlighted the importance of attitude and the desire to teach. He referred to the emotional and mental composition of the individual teacher and proclaimed as follows:

1.   The teacher must always be projected into the thinking of others.
2.   The teacher must do so not in the sense of command or ordering students to do things, but as a sympathetic and understanding guide.

What Thorndike is saying here is that, emotionally and mentally, the teacher should be patient and willing to show and guide patiently the students until they have acquired the necessary competence. In addition, the teacher must learn how to transfer his interest from the subject being taught to the students. The teacher must make central in his thinking, in what the students are learning rather than what he is teaching.

ABILITY TO DEVELOP GOOD PERSONAL RELATIONS

It is a well-established principle of learning that positive personal relationships between the teacher and the students contribute to adequate learning (Knowles, 1973; Miller & Rose, 1975; Knox, 1981; Thorndike, 2000).

Students generally, respond very quickly to genuine interest. If they believe that their teacher likes them and has confidence in them, they will generally have a greater desire to achieve. What we are saying here is, when a teacher has good interpersonal relations with his students, he can require and get much more achievement from them in the long run than one who is disked, resented, or not respected for his ability.

Thus, it could be said that, a teacher must work in harmony with his colleagues, his students; the supervisors and the administrators of his school. It is only when the teacher is able to demonstrate the willingness to work in harmony with each of the above groups that he will earn respect from his associates, the students and his superiors.

CONCLUSION

It is important to note that, however hard we try, and however much we think what we do is perfect, other people might not share our views. There will always be some who are dissatisfied with what we do or wish that we did things differently. This, however, does not prevent us from trying our best.

The effective teacher is not a perfect individual. Therefore, in addition to his or her best, the following are suggested:

1. Be friendly with everybody including students and your associates.
2. Cooperate with other teachers that work with either in the areas of instructional and non-instructional areas.
3. Take part in social activities such as recreational and other social programs.
4. Compliment achievement of others from time to time.
5. Be considerate of other people's feelings. Since we do not know how others feel about many things, we should be cautious in situations that may prove embarrassing.
6. Maintain good personal appearance; and
7. Be professional and competent as an educated person. Be intellectually curious, think critically, weigh issues dispassionately and be tolerant.

CHAPTER EIGHTEEN

VOCATIONAL EDUCATION IN NIGERIA

ONI, C.S. PH.D

INTRODUCTION

Vocational education is not a new concept in Nigerian education. Before the advent of Colonial influence in Africa, there was a traditional educational system prevalent in African societies. In the traditional educational system in Nigeria, children learning by doing, that is to say, children were involved in practical farming, fishing, weaving, cooking, carving, knitting, painting, wood making and so on (Fafunwa, 1974).

A vocation in general terms can simply mean one's occupation or work, or one's means of livelihood. In the ordinary sense, the term vocation can be used for a lower level of job training. In Nigeria and other part of Africa, such lower level jobs include carpentry, bricklaying, plumbing, painting, cabinet-making, motor mechanics, installation mechanics, welding, basket making, weaving, blacksmithing, electricians and son on.

Vocational education includes technical education. While vocational education provides for the training or retraining designed to prepare individuals to enter into a paid employment in any recognized occupation, technical education on the other hand, in common practice, is composed of theoretical and practical instruction. Such instruction is generally given to those who need to be employed in commerce and industry or in any type of enterprise, which involves the use of tools and other machinery for their operational services

(Adetoro, 1985). The operational services of such industry could include production, distribution of goods or any other technical related works.

Vocational education is a highly useful education because its occupational content offers the trainees the opportunity to acquire skills, attitudes, interests, and the knowledge which they need to perform technologically and economically the job that is beneficial not only to them but to their society.

Vocational education, in Nigeria, unfortunately however, has not performed its potential role of technological and economic transformation of our nation because of certain factors. Such factors, which are contained in the history of vocational education, are reviewed in this article as follow:

1.   The general masses perception of the education
2.   The inadequate funding of the programs by Federal and State government, and
3.   The constant low enrolment of students is the programs.

In conjunction with the above factors, this chapter examines the Nigerian manpower needs and the overall enrolment of students in vocational programs throughout the nation.

HISTORICAL DEVELOPMENT OF VOCATIONAL EDUCATION IN NIGERIA

The Nigerian Government, as far back as 1942, according to Coleman (1963), was not unaware of the needs for a system of education in which the general and the literary instruction is balanced by a progressive development of technical and vocational education. In the 1900, for example, as Coleman 1963 put it, the Lagos Board of Education passed the following resolutions about education in general.

1.   That it is not possible for our schools to produce really good results unless we are less apathetic about education; and
2.   That unless we provide a comprehensive scheme of public instruction, which shall not only supply the wants of a clerkly class, but should also prepare youths for husbandry and handicrafts (Coleman, 1963, p. 131).

In spite of the above resolution to balance the general and the literacy instruction in our educational system, no important steps were taken to redress the lack of balance especially with regards to vocational/technical education. For example, by 1913, only seven schools in Lagos and the then Southern Provinces offered any form of technical or vocational training. The schools were the two Government schools at Bonny and Warri, and the Hope Waddle Institute, Calabar. The other was girls' schools in Lagos. In 1934, Dr. Nnamdi Azikiwe who rose to become the first President of the republic of Nigeria in 1960, made a strong complaint about the lack of opportunities for technically trained Nigerians when he stated that:

(1) Neither the European Government would employ them, nor would European private enterprises, nor would the missions with their limited budget.

(2) That these Africans lack sufficient capital to enter into business. Therefore they continue the cycle of teaching others to teach agriculture and industrial education (Azikwe, 1934, p. 147).

The serious neglect for vocational/technical education in Nigeria continued up to the end of the Second World War. However, in the 1946 Ten Year Development Plan, it was proposed that three trade centers be established-one at Yaba, one at Enugu and one at Zaria or Kaduna in the Northern provinces.

Although, the proposed vocational/technical institutions were duly established in various Nigerian provinces, the facilities for technical education and the rate of progress were inadequate.

Besides, very little attention was paid to the higher technical and professional levels. For example, the Zaria centers were not established until late January 1952 while Yaba center was established later.

Ten years later, the Northern regional government's training school at Bukuru was established to offer a three-year course in technical training leading to the award of the city and Guild Certificate of the London Institute. A similar center was established in Kano, Ilorin and Kaduna later in 1964.

In spite of the positive governmental efforts to establish vocational/technical institutions during the early 1960s, the Skapaki reports in 1966, affirmed that there certainly had been no viable attempts to improve vocational and technical education in Nigeria at that time. The Skapki report (1966), reveals that vocational/technical programs in Nigeria were faced with problems such as finance, personnel, facilities and inadequate supply of program materials and equipment.

Emanating from various reports and from various suggestions on how to improve and to effectively establish good institutions for the development of vocational/technical programs, the Nigerian National Policy in Education 1981, listed the aims of vocational/technical education as follows:

1. TO provide trained manpower in applied science technology and commence particularly at sub-professional grades;

2. To provide technical knowledge and vocational skills necessary for agricultural, industry, commercial and economic development.
3. To provide people who can apply scientific knowledge to the improvement and solution of environmental problems for the use and convenience of man;
4. To give training and impact the necessary skills leading to the production of craftsmen, technicians and other skilled personnel who will be enterprising and self-reliant, and
5. To enable our young ones and women to have an intelligent understanding of the increasing complexity of technology (NPE, 1981, p. 28).

Ever since the National Policy on Education was formulated, several public and private vocation and technical institutions have been established in various states in the country. In addition, the Nigerian Fourth National Development plan (NFNDP, 1981–85), also reveals that our government at all levels, have recognized the importance of vocational/technical education by calling for the effective implementation of vocational programs in our secondary and post-secondary institutions.

The awareness of the importance of vocational/technical education by our government in the 1980s as a necessary tool for the economic and technological development is vital. Regrettably however, even at the present time 2005, vocation education has not performed its potential role of our economic and technological transformation. One of the major reasons for the inadequate performance is due to ineffective organization of vocational programs in our institution.

VOCATIONAL PROGRAMS

In 1930s and 40s, most Boys Vocational Institutions in Nigeria offered Wood Sawing, Carpentry, Joinery, Coopering, Engineering, Telegraphy, Printing, Tailoring and Gardening. In the Girls Schools, Domestic Economy was taught in its various branches. Also, Plain Needlework, Washing and Ironing, Baking of Bread, Preparation of Native Foodstuff, and fancy Needlework were taught (Thorp and Marlow, 1930). New Programs were introduced into other vocational/technical institutions in the 1950s. For example, with the establishment of the Nigerian College of Arts, Science and Technology, as a federal institution with branches at Ibadan, Enugu and Zaria in 1952, technical education programs such as Architecture, Land Surveying, Pharmacy, Accountancy and Secretarial Studies were set up.

The establishment of Polytechnic Institutions across the nation in the 1970s and 80s, has also become one avenue for producing the much desired vocational/ technical manpower for the eventual technological and economic development of the nation. As indicated by the Nigerian Fourth National Development Plan (NFNDP, 1981–85), more than 50,000 students were enrolled in various vocational/technical education programs during the 1984–85 academic sessions across the states in the country. In conjunction with the above student enrolment figure, the Federal Republic of Nigeria Social Statistic (FRNSS, 1985), also reports the overall enrolment for vocational/technical programs for the 1984/85 academic year to be 46,083 students.

In spite of the huge number of student enrolment in our vocational/technical programs, our national manpower needs for 1984/85 academic session, as revealed by (NFNDP, 1981–85), was estimated to be over 60,000 professional and technical occupations. And, only one third of the 50,000 total enrolments of students in our vocational/technical program during the 1984/85 academic session, graduated. That is, about 16,667 students (33%) of the total enrolment graduated. Thus, the 16,667 graduates accounts for only 28% of our nations' manpower needs for the 1984/85 academic year (FRNSS, 1985 p. 79).

About N2.2 billion (Naira) was allocated for University Education by Federal Government of Nigeria during 2002/2003 fiscal year while only N9.5 million (Naira) was allocated for Vocational Technical Education, (PBMO, 2004).

In conjunction with the inadequate enrolment of students and graduates required to meet our nation's manpower needs, Nigerian Federal government continues to allocate insufficient funds for vocational/technical education programs. For example, in the 1989 Federal Budget allocation for education, a total of N1.94 billion (Naira), was allocated for education. From this amount, about N800 million was allocated for Primary education while only about N600 million (Naira) was allocated for vocational-technical education (Daily Times, 1/10/89, p.10).

The aforementioned financial inadequacy, coupled with the inadequate student enrolment and graduates from our vocational/technical institutions, thus explain why the Nigerian government even after forty-four years of independence, has failed to satisfy our national manpower needs. To this day, the initial bias against, and the disdain for vocational/technical education is still evident. Students into vocational/technical colleges in the country reflect this bias against vocational/technical education in the enrolment response. And unless the Nigerian government at the Federal, State and Local levels can adequately allocate funds for the effective planning and development of our vocational/

technical programs, it will be highly difficult as a nation to improve the current image of vocational/technical education in Nigeria.

CHAPTER NINETEEN

PROMOTING SOCIETAL DEVELOPMENT THROUGH AN INTERDISCIPLINARY APPROACH TO CONTENT SELECTION AND ORGANIZATION IN THE TEACHING OF MATHEMATICS AND LANGUAGE SKILLS

DR. E. O. OLOYEDE AND DR. (MRS.) Y. A. AJIBADE

INTRODUCTION

Societies by their nature do not remain static, as there is always the possibility of progress or retrogression. Progress in any society is however, not automatic. Certain steps need to be taken to ensure that the growth process expected is realized. If these steps are not taken, no growth will occur and the society concerned will remain in a state of underdevelopment. Steps to ensure growth in a given society cut across the political, the economic and the social.

In this chapter, focus is placed on social steps with particular emphasis on education. An attempt is made to discuss ways of bringing about growth in a society like Nigeria through better teaching of language skills, which are expected to contribute to improved learning of mathematics. This issue is examined using an interdisciplinary approach to the teaching of mathematics and English, the medium of instruction in Nigerian secondary schools.

This is considered necessary given the importance of mathematics in today's global setting. The effect of language on learning has been a research topic for years with little impact on actual classroom practice.

This study concludes with practical implications for the teaching of mathematical concepts, within an English language framework.

THE CONCEPT OF DEVELOPMENT

The concept of development itself implies a progression from a simpler or lower level to a more advanced, mature or complex form or stage. Development is conceived as the determination of the best techniques for applying a new device or process to production of goods and services. The modernization paradigm, which supports an earlier work on development, considers development as a social growth process with societies moving through stages from traditional to transitional and modern.

Newer models of development tend to link underdevelopment to factors such as contextual and structural inequalities, resource control and deprivation rather than to inherent abilities. Another development model being proposed is one that emphasizes self-esteem, self-reliance and support for indigenous values (Opubor, 2000). Ndoye (2002) deduces that the reductionist-economistic approach to development, hitherto in operation, is now giving way to social and human dimensions, which have now become the driving forces of development.

This shift in paradigm is influenced partially by the United Nation's Millennium Development Goals adopted in 2000 at the Millennium Summit. These goals are to:
- eradicate extreme poverty and hunger;
- achieve universal primary education;
- promote gender equality and empower women;
- reduce child mortality;
- improve maternal health;
- combat HIV/AIDS, malaria and other diseases;
- ensure environmental sustainability;

• develop a global partnership for development, which sets objectives for aid, international trade and debt reduction.

EDUCATION AND SOCIETAL DEVELOPMENT

The importance of education in promoting societal development is obvious. Education, in this approach, has become a central issue, a major key to the door of progress. For a society's development, therefore, its educational system must be well looked into. This implies that no nation can rise above its educational level. According to Ndoye (2002)

"every international initiative now places education at the heart of the process of shaping human capital, economic growth, equitable redistribution ... and the promotion of human rights within and between generations".

Education leads to both linear and horizontal development. Education, like development, needs to be well planned for it to effectively affect lives in any society.

THE AFRICAN EXPERIENCE

In spite of the Education for All (EFA) by 2015, discussion and research works have consistently revealed poor standards of education in African countries. For example, Novicki (www.un.org/ecosocdev/geninfo/afrec/vol11no4/educat. htm) and Borishade (2002) note that a majority of those who should be in school are not there in spite of the EFA drive. During the Conference of the Ministers of Education of African Member States (2002) discussants opined that the quality of education in Africa was below expectation. The need to improve the relevance and quality of education was reiterated. The role of literacy and education in Science and Technology in alleviating the problem of poverty and health believed to plague African countries was also discussed.

It was further noted at the conference that the area of Science and Technology was one with the highest shortfall of human resources in Africa. Consequently, the entire human resource potential of Africa should be tapped for economic and sustainable economic and social development through Science and Technology Education (STE). The interdisciplinary approach being adopted in this study is in line with the UNESCO proposed action, which aims at promoting STE in Africa through networking and capacity building at promoting girls' participation in STE.

THE POSITION OF MATHEMATICS IN SCIENCE AND TECHNOLOGY EDUCATION

Knowledge of mathematics is universally accepted as indispensable for the scientific and technological development of a nation. As the world continues its globalization process through technological invention and computerization, the impact of mathematics in the development of any society becomes more obvious and consequently an issue of concern for those who value education.

Mathematical knowledge infiltrates all areas of life including banking and finance, accounting, business, economics and even the liberal arts contrary to expectations. In today's global world, science and technology, with mathematical knowledge as basis, is an area that must be adequately emphasized. It is needless to say that whatever language used as medium to pass across mathematical skills has a role to play in the understanding of the subject.

LANGUAGE, MATHEMATICS LEARNING AND THE NIGERIAN CONTEXT.

Problems of the language used as the medium of instruction can create obstacles to understanding in every subject. Orton (1994) notes the fact that pupils experience problems when learning any subject, including mathematics. He further states that problems of language are not unique to children of any particular country. Literature reveals that mathematics-language related problems arise from the linguistic form and semantic structure of language (Riley, Greeno and Heller, 1983; Li, 1990; De Corte and Verschaffel, 1991; Orton and Wain 1994). Other researchers such as Jones (1982), Zepp (1982), Thorburn & Orton (1990) discuss problems associated with the grammatical structure of language and its relationship with mathematics understanding or its lack of understanding.

It has been discussed over the years that subjects are better learnt at school, in the initial stages, through the first languages of the society in question (UNESCO, 2003; Fafunwa, Macauley & Sokoya (1989); Adetula, 1990). Nevertheless, in a country like Nigeria where the official language is different from the first language in any sector of the society, a transition to the official language from the first language is required at some point in time. However, there are unanswered questions relating to when and how transition should be made to learning mathematics in a second language. Though the National Policy on Education (NPE, 1998) goes a step further in its latest revision to state that transition to English as a medium of instruction for all subjects will be made in primary four, it does not state how and this usually gives teachers room to continue teaching in the first language indefinitely. As expected, this affects teaching at later stages of the educational system.

As injurious to learning as these issues are, Orton and Wain (1994) note that research on language and mathematics learning has focused mainly on identifying problem issues rather than at providing guidance for effective intervention in the classroom. Unanswered questions, according to them, show that there still remains the potential for a lot of experimentation and variation with the choice of language to be used, when and how to use the first or second language within the privacy of the classroom.

In Nigeria, at the secondary school level, learners are expected to have switched from the first language to the official language, which is English. In spite of the policy statements made in the NPE (1998) regarding the relationship between language as medium of instruction and other subjects, results obtained in the various subjects including English fall short of expectations. It is pertinent at this juncture to find out how the English language used as medium of instruction at this stage could be used to promote rather than hinder understanding in mathematics even in a second language setting. To achieve this, focus is placed on mathematics—language relationship at the level of vocabulary development.

Otterburn and Nicholson (1976) found out, while investigating school children's understanding of a variety of mathematical terms, that there were many mathematical words teachers use that children were unable to explain. According to Orton (1994: 131–132), it is important that children are given help with the language, which they are going to be expected to use in discussing and generally processing ideas, in order to facilitate the learning of mathematical ideas. He goes on to make suggestions such as introducing new ideas, words and symbols through speech, written work and discussions; using vocabulary activities such as simple word search based on the mathematical topic of interest; elementary crossword used to attach words to their meanings; unscrambling words; matching a list of words with a list of meanings or a set of pictures; selecting the best description for a word from a number of alternatives; or a mixture of activities. He concludes by saying that using lesson time for such activities might be considered a nuisance until one realizes that coping with the vocabulary is an important part of learning the ideas. While the mathematics teacher might be of the opinion that setting time aside to teach mathematics-related vocabulary is a waste of time, the language teacher by virtue of his/ her profession should be ready to do so. The language teacher's duty is to help facilitate language learning irrespective of the register of the vocabulary item. As observed by Orton & Wain (1994) "the language used by a mathematics teacher, a textbook writer, and an examiner, involves the use of particular structures or grammatical patterns associated with the mathematical register".

It is therefore expected of not only the mathematics, but also the English textbook in Nigeria, to cover elements of language necessary for the understanding of mathematical concepts. Focus is placed in this study on the English class as an avenue for initial treatment of mathematical terms using the suggested activities above as well as others.

CONTENT SELECTION AND ORGANIZATION OF MATHEMATICAL TERMS FOR THE USE OF THE ENGLISH TEACHER

For learning not to be fragmented, the English Teacher needs to be guided in the task of teaching mathematical terms. The textbook, as an instructional resource, usually helps the teacher in selecting and organizing content to be taught in the classroom. One of the recommended English language textbooks for secondary schools—The *New Syllabus Effective English for Junior Secondary Schools* BK. 1 by Michael Montgomery, M.O. Okebukola and J.O. Bisong was examined in line with the suggested glossary of mathematical terms by Soyemi and Jegede (2000). The tables below show the findings:

Table 1:   Mathematical Words in English Textbook

Glossary of Mathematical Terms	Number of Mathematical Words in English Textbook	Percentage
1, 100	135	12.3%

Table 2:   Unit by Unit Analysis of Mathematical Words

Unit	Number of Mathematical Words	Percentage
1	6	4%
2	3	2%
3	8	6%
4	2	1%
5	8	6%

6	11	8%
7	7	5%
8	17	13%
9	7	5%
10	11	8%
11	14	10%
12	7	5%
13	11	8%
14	15	11%
15	3	2%
16	5	4%

Table 3:   Percentage of Mathematical Words Requiring Everyday Meanings

Number of Mathematical Words	Number of Words Requiring Everyday Meanings	Percentage
135	119	88%

Table 4:   Percentage of Mathematical Words Found under Vocabulary Development

Number of Mathematical Words	Number of Words Found under Vocabulary Development	%	Numbers of Words used in Explaining Words under Vocabulary Development	%
135	1	0.74%	15	11%

From the tables above, one finds in Table 1 that there is a certain percentage of mathematical terms included in the English language textbook examined. The adequacy in terms of the number included is obviously inadequate while evaluation of the type of words used is outside the scope of this study. In Table 2, one finds that there is no unit without a number of mathematical terms, no matter how few. Table 3 reveals that a larger percentage of the mathematical terms included in the textbook requires everyday meanings for them to be understood in the context of the English language class. Table 4 shows that the mathematical words included in the textbook are not all found under vocabulary development where words whose meanings need to be understood are given special attention.

IMPLICATIONS FOR AN INTERDISCIPLINARY APPROACH TO THE TEACHING OF MATHEMATICS AND LANGUAGE SKILLS.

The English language teacher faced with the task of teaching English in a society like Nigeria where it is used as a medium of instruction should bear the following in mind:

1. He/she needs to be very familiar with the textbook recommended for the particular class to be handled in order to use it correctly and maximally for the linguistic development of the learners.
2. In preparing each unit, the teacher should not only concentrate only on words that are immediately useful to him/her in a particular lesson.
3. The teacher should endeavor to teach both the everyday meanings as well as the technical meanings of mathematical terms bearing in mind that the mathematics teacher might not be a good English teacher even of mathematical terms.
4. The English language teacher should not concentrate only on words found under vocabulary development when meanings of words are to be taught. Very useful words are very many times put in passages, instructions, explanations and so on.
5. The English language teacher needs to work closely with the mathematics teacher because the work of the English teacher in an educational system like Nigeria's has a lot of impact on that of the mathematics teacher and teachers of other subjects.
6. While encouraging teachers of science and mathematics, it should be borne in mind that there can be no true technological development without the input of the language teacher.

SUGGESTIONS FOR FURTHER STUDY

For this study to be as comprehensive as it should be, the following are suggested for further study:

1. Similar analysis should be done with other recommended text-books to cover the entire Junior Secondary School (JSS) and Senior Secondary School (SSS) periods.
2. Similar analysis could be done in other subject areas apart from mathematics.
3. An experimental study should be carried out involving the language teacher in the manner proposed in this study.

CHAPTER TWENTY

ENVIRONMENTAL DEGRADATION: A NEED FOR PUBLIC ENLIGHTENMENT.

OGEDENGBE P.S. AND OSUNTOGUN D.A

INTRODUCTION

A general look at the Nigerian environment today, reveals a progressive reduction in quality as a result of indiscriminate dumping of wastes (especially toxic wastes), trade effluents, oil spills and other hazardous substances. Environmental degradation occurs as a result of human activities and get more pronounced with population explosion particularly in our cities. Population increase brings about more sewage, more solid wastes, more fuel being burnt, more fertilizers and insecticides being used to produce more food etc. Environmental degradation can also result from oil exploration with it attendants toxic properties of hydrocarbon constituents which can bring about gradual extermination of aquatic and animal life.

The advent of mining and industrial revolution in Nigeria came with its antecedent activities like extraction, harvesting, processing, distribution and marketing. These finished Industrial and agricultural products are purchased and consumed by Nigerian households and the wastes are thrown into the environment.

Industrial revolution coupled with rapid urbanization in Nigeria has accelerated the rate of environmental degradation in the country. This chapter tries to focus on the need for public enlightenment as a way of controlling environmental degradation in Nigeria.

THE STATEMENT OF PROBLEM

The rate of degradation that faces our environment particularly in the Niger Delta and some urban areas today in Nigeria is alarming hence urgent and adequate concern should be shown and steps taken to address this menace.

Environmental degradation can occur through biological, chemical or physical means. Biodegradation is the inherent ability of natural decay processes to break natural compounds to their constituent elements and compounds for the assimilation in and by biological renewal cycles.

Man's survival depends solely on the environment and as a result his effort to utilize this opportunity through exploration and exploitation often results in environmental degradation. This occurs from an undesirable alteration in the physical, chemical, social and biological property of the land, air and water, which constitute the environment.

Arising from the above discussion, the chapter tries to find solutions to the following questions.

What are the causes of environmental degradation?

How can this menace be controlled?

How can public enlightenment be used to solve the problem of environmental degradation?

These and other problems are what the chapter intends to address.

SCOPE AND OBJECTIVE

This chapter tries to examine the importance of public enlightenment in curbing environmental degradation problems in Nigeria. In achieving this, it sets to examine the major causes of environmental degradation and ways of controlling them.

ENVIRONMENT

Section 38 of the Federal Environmental Protection Agency Act (FEPA) interprets environment to "… include water, air, land and all plants and human beings or animals living therein and the interrelationships which exist among these or any of them". Rau and Wooten (1986) defined environment as "the whole complex of physical, social, cultural, economic and aesthetic factors, which affect individuals and communities and ultimately_determines their form, character, relationship and survival". The duo of Rau and Wooten (1986) categorized the dimensions of the environment into four:

1. The Physical
This includes land and climate, vegetation, wildlife, the surrounding land uses and the physical character of an arena, infrastructure/public services, air, noise and water pollution.

2. The Social
This includes community facilities and the character of community facilities and services and the character of communities.

3. The Aesthetic
That is scenic areas, vistas, views including architectural character of buildings.

4. The Economy
This consists of employment, land ownership pattern and land values.

Generally, environment can be viewed as surroundings, especially the material and spiritual influences which, affect the growth, development and existence of a living being.

DEGRADATION

The word degradation connotes reducing the quality of a particular thing. Environmental degradation is the process of reducing the quality of the environment through biological, chemical or physical means. Reduction in the quality of the environment through pollution is a form of environmental degradation. Chemical degradation of the environment can be induced by a number of gases especially the causative gases that emanate from gas flaring and other atmospheric emissions. Heat and light can also cause thermal and photo degradation e.g. photochemical smogs.

ENVIRONMENTAL PROBLEMS

(a) Water, forest and land degradation due to human encroachment;
(b) Urban environmental degradation arising from pressure from rural migrants and provision of inadequate facilities;
(c) Inadequate water supply and sanitation;
(d) Coastal degradation especially caused by excessive erosion and flooding;
(e) Coastal and marine pollution largely by oil exploration production and marketing activities both in the coastal areas and offshore.
(f) Air pollution caused by industrial waste emissions;
(g) Pollution of waterways by both community generated and industrial wastes.
(h) Noise pollution in our cities.

ENVIRONMENTAL POLLUTION

Pollution is the unfavorable alteration of our surrounding, largely as a by-product of man activities or actions through direct or indirect effect of changes in energy patterns, radiation level, chemical and physical condition and abundance of organisms.

Biologist however defines pollution as the addition to the environment of any material, which has detrimental effect on the ecosystem. It can be natural or man-made, while the natural degradation results from volcanic eruption, sea spray, vapor phase, out-gasing, e.t.c. the man-made (anthropographic) environmental degradation stems from environmental pollution through burning of fossil fuel, firewoods, metal mining and processing, agricultural activities (fertilizers), oil spills, industrial emission and wastes, nuclear reactors & bomb test, and bush burning, among others.

The Federal Environmental Protection Agency Views environmental pollution as man-made or man-aided alteration of chemical, physical or biological quality of the environment to the extent that it is detrimental to the environment or beyond acceptable limits. Environmental pollution occurs mainly due to human activities and it gets more pronounced with population explosion in most of the urban centers in Nigeria. Oil exploration and exploitation coupled with technological advancement always have consequential effect of environmental degradation.

Environmental pollution from oil exploitation arises mainly from upstream operations in the form of blowouts, geo-thermal stream, gas flaring and oil

spills and upstream operations transporting petroleum products via pipelines
to storage depots spotted all over the Country.

BLOWOUT

A blowout is the sudden and violent escape of gas into the atmosphere. This
occurs when the pressure built around the oil well becomes heavier than the
wells hydrostatic weight. This alters the composition and character of the
atmosphere thereby degrading the environment. This environmental degradation through blowout is a very common feature associated with drilling.

GEO-THERMAL STREAM

This is the stream emitted into the atmosphere in the normal process of oil
exploitation through drilling. This stream consists of hydrogen sulphide,
methane and ammonia. The hydrogen sulphide converts into sulphur dioxide
when it reaches the earth surface, and it has harmful effects on all living things
including man. Ammonia on the other hand combines with some other compounds in the atmosphere to cause acid rain.

GAS FLARING

This is another major source of environmental degradation. It is the process of
burning unutilized associated gases into the atmosphere. This has damaging
consequences on the ecosystem. Economic trees and cash crops within a radius
of the gas flare cities are charmed and wither out over years. The heat, noise
and stench generated by flare make life unbearable for the most communities, as the residents can neither sleep comfortably at night nor in the day. The
farmlands are hot throughout the year hence the healthy growth to agricultural
corps is discouraged.

Gas flaring has negative impact on corrugated iron sheets through corro-
sion as a result of acid rains. It also depletes the Ozone layer in the sky.

OIL SPILLS

This is the leakage or discharge of petroleum into the surface of inland or coastal
waters. Oil on water surfaces is harmful to many forms of aquatic life because

it prevents sufficient amount of sunlight from penetrating and also reduces the level of dissolved oxygen in the water. Crude oil also renders gills and feathers ineffective so that fish and birds may die as a result of direct contact with it.

The effects of oil spills on the immediate environment are readily obvious but their long-term impact on the ecosystem of an affected area is more difficult to evaluate.

Water pollution is any man-made alteration of the chemical, physical or biological quality of water, which results in an unacceptable depreciation of the utility or environmental value of water. Water pollution can be as a result of solid debris, hot water from factory and chemical contaminants from industrial waste and oil spills.

Air pollution covers those pollutants that are emitted into the atmosphere usually from land as gases or particulate, which directly or indirectly degrade or adversely affect the physical and biological system of the environment. The addition of this unwanted air born matter changes the composition of the atmosphere possibly harming lives and affecting materials. These pollutants range from visible particulates (smoke and dust) to invisible and odorless gases (carbon monoxide). Air pollution stems from automobile exhaust, bush burning, and chemical smog, among others. These emit carbon monoxide, which combines with haemoglobin, to impair oxygen transport. Air pollutants contaminate the upper atmosphere, alter weather and climatic conditions, cause global warming "green house effect" and ozone layer depletion.

WAYS OF CONTROLLING ENVIRONMENTAL DEGRADATION

A legal maxim (ibi jus ubi remendium), which means that for every harm, there ought to be a remedy should be invoked for controlling the menace of environmental degradation. This system will be very effective in view of the fact that man-made environmental degradation is our focus.

Since environmental degradation has become an established phenomenon in the Niger Delta and urban centers in Nigeria, it is imperative on every stakeholder to put in place measures to avoid and combat such problems. Proper legal framework to checkmate environmental degradation as a result of oil operations should be put in place by the Government.

The wastes that results in environmental degradation can be recycled in order to make them useful thereby reducing their negative effects on the environment. To be able to control environmental degradation effectively, the

various environmental laws should be reviewed and made more responsive to
our peculiar environmental challenges. In the same line of thought, Ikhariale
(1998) observed that the existing statutes are inadequate to the extent that
they did not fully appreciate the magnitude of the risk to which their violation
posed to society in the short and long-run. Under these laws, environmental
offences such as pollution are classified as 'misdemeanor', which attracts paltry
penalty. These inadequacies in the environmental laws gave room for the incessant problems of oil spillage in the Niger Delta and environmental pollution in
the cities with the consequent disruption of the ecosystem.

The remedy to the damage done to the environment as provided in the various environmental laws is inadequate since where it is possible to estimate the
physical damages to farmlands and marine life, it may not be possible to quan-
tify the damage done to the Ozone layer, the ecosystem and the potential health
hazards, which can only manifest in future years especially among the generations unborn. Very often, when environmental degradation occurs through oil
spills, paltry compensation or damages are awarded to individuals and communities on physical losses without compensation for environmental losses.

Cleaning up action should be enforced in order to restore the environment
to its original state, even when compensation has been paid by the person, or
company, that degraded the environment. Environmental consciousness is a
vital instrument for combating environmental degradation problems. People
should be enlightened to know that environmental degradation is not only
inimical to individuals or communities, but an intractable harm to the society
at large, and has become a global phenomenon. The atmosphere is very vital
for the survival of man and other living beings, by providing air for respiration
and photosynthesis, shading them from dangerous particles and rays. It is also
a medium for air navigation. To achieve a clean air situation, there is need to
designate and map National air control zone, provide standards for factories,
licensing and registering all major industrial air pollutants and monitor their
compliance with standards for abatement.

For the control of noise pollution, noise standards and acoustic guarantees
can be set up; prescribe permissible noise level in noise prone industries and
construction sites and ensure installation of noise dampers; provide guidelines
for the control of air craft noise and set up quiet zones in game parks and
reserves, among others. Energy consumption increases in the urban areas as a
result of industrialization. The negative impact of energy production and use
on the environment can be checked by promoting safe and pollution free operations in energy production and use; monitoring and controlling the level of
noxious by—products of energy production and use and to reduce the "green

house" effects; monitoring oil spill contingency plans; monitoring and assessing the environmental protection programs in upstream and downstream activities in the petroleum industry exploration, production, refining, petrochemicals transportation and marketing; encouraging re-injection and utilization of produced gases to prevent the adverse environmental impact of gas flares, licensing of energy waste disposal sites.

Water resources management can be achieved by considering the environmental impact of water resources development at the planning stages; efficient supply and usage of water; preventing contamination and depletion of water resources; using river basin concepts in water management.

CONLUSION

For the effectiveness of the above measures for controlling environmental degradation in Nigeria, there is need for public enlightenment so that individuals, corporate bodies and government agencies will know their roles in keeping the environment healthy since Man's survival depends solely on it. This public enlightenment will make them know their roles in keeping the environment. This will arouse environmental consciousness among Nigerians, which will make them know the likely effects of their activities on the environment.

If everybody is made to be aware of the importance of a healthy environment, then Nigerians will be mindful of what they do that may likely affect the environment negatively thereby minimizing the man made environmental degradation which is the major focus of the chapter. Public enlightenment will drum it in the ears of Nigerians that whatever affects the environment negatively will also have negative effect on their own lives. Environmental impact assessment should be made compulsory before any development is carried out so that the mitigating measures are provided. Public enlightenment can also help in this direction of achieving a healthy environment. Conclusively, this enlightenment will throw light on the importance of the environment to human, plant and animal lives; the activities of man that contribute negatively to the environment.

CHAPTER TWENTY-ONE

THE EMERGING ROLES OF ADULT EDUCATORS IN ERADICATING CULTISM AND VIOLENCE IN INSTITUTIONS OF HIGHER LEARNING

AKANDE J.O. AND OSHUNTOGUN D.A.

INTRODUCTION

It is no longer news, that most of our institutions of higher learning in Nigeria are permeated with the evils of cultism, violence, examination malpractices, killing, maiming and raping. Unfortunately, these ever-existing problems multiply with time. Obviously, the upsurge of secret cult activities in particular with the corollaries of arson, brutality and dehumanization have turned the Nigerian institutions of higher learning, which are supposed to be citadel of academic excellence, to direful and formidable human abattoirs. It is on this note that Ezeah (2001) aptly submits that, the preponderance of secret cults in institutions of higher learning in Nigeria has not only become an anathema but a negation of the ideals for which the institutions stand for. He laments that our tertiary institutions are gradually sliding into "war theatres" and gangsterism as a result of cultism. Ofordile (2001) and Ifeoma (2001) corroborating this view, maintain that secret societies have taken control of our higher institutions constituting a threat to the stability and peace of the Nigerian Society. It is therefore a well-directed effort, to eradicate the menace of cultism and violence in the Nigerian institutions of higher learning.

Obviously, observations show that quite a few of the adolescents and young adults are initiated into cultism and cultic rituals. Ofordile (2001) reporting Emerson and Syron (1995) contends that the adolescents' engagement in cultism and violence is arrantly hazardous. This is based on the assumption that the adolescents always go on rampage revolting against the existing culture, political and religious structures. Apparently, such obnoxious acts pose untold crises and challenges in the institutions of higher learning. It seems as if the parents are incapable of curbing cult practices among the adolescents and the youths, a situation depicting the need for the interventions of various organizations in the society. This brings to the fore the emerging roles of adult educators to help in reducing the incessant incidents of cultism in Nigeria.

Apparently, the broad concept of adult education stresses the importance of serving all in need of more knowledge, information, skills and other learning (Obanewa, 1999). Hence, it is a kind of education that embraces non-formal education, lifelong education, adult basic education, literacy, numeracy, functional-work-oriented, post-literacy education, training civic education, conscientization, liberal education, community education and development, out-of-school education, extension education such as agricultural extension, continuing education, recurrent education and so on (Bown and Tomori, 1999). Its point of contact with cultism and violence is that it could be used as a veritable instrument to eradicate menaces of cultism and for the promotion of better citizenship in the society.

Therefore, this study examines the concepts and challenges of cultism and violence couple with the challenges of cultism in Nigeria educational institutions. This is with a view to exploring the role of adult counseling and education in curbing the menace of secret cults and violence in higher educational institutions in Nigeria.

The Concepts of Secret Cult and Violence:
Secret Cult:

Cultism and violence are dual evils rocking most of the higher institutions of learning in recent times. Ifeoma (2001) asserts that members of secret cults straddle the whole spectrum of University life. This implies that there is no single disciplinary area that is not infested by secret cultists. The question now is what is cultism or secret cult?

According to Ofordile (2001) quoting Enroth (1979), the word cult itself has been variously applied to groups involved in beliefs and practices just off the beat of traditional religion ns, making exploratory excursions into non-Western philosophical practices, and to groups involving intense relationships between followers and a powerful idea or leader. This corroborates the view of van Baalen (1962) quoted in Ofordile (2001) describing cultism as the unpaid bills of the church. This implies that cultism came into being as a false, derisive and impudent imitation of Christianity. And Buckland (1988), reported in Ofordile (2001), was right in presenting a life-like image of cultism as an amusing caricature of Christianity. Okirika (2001) defines cult as an organization of a group of initiates who are devoted to some system of religious worship made up of rituals and other practices to a figure of a god or saint who they revere and pay homage to owing to their beliefs and doctrines.

Also, Ezeah (2001) defines a cult as a religious movement that usually involve the introduction of totally new religious ideas and principles. From ethical perspective, cult could be defined as a group, which follows dominant leader, accepts his claims, doctrines and dogma and obeys a set of determined command (Beck (1995). On the other hand, Eyibe (1995), identifies secret cult as a wicked and hedonistic association of mediocre students whose aim is to eliminate, intimidate, frighten, terrorize, hurt, or even destroy fellow students and their staff because they see no authority which they can respect.

No matter how perceived, it is obvious that secret cults are unlawful associations of malefactors, gangsters and fugitives. Members of secret cults are antisocial and always pernicious. It is on this note that Appel (1983), contends that cults set themselves apart in showing varying degrees of hostility towards the outside world. They are led by charismatic and authoritarian figures. Their obnoxious behaviors, mode of dressing, language, controls of communication, authoritarian rules and prohibitions portray them as villains, whose hearts are blackened with evil. Hence, they are often formidable and ghastly, orchestrating violence and commotion in the society. From every indication, it is apparent that the secret cult societies constitute themselves as pain in the neck and pea in the shoe in the Nigeria's tertiary institutions.

Rudin (1990) described some characteristics of secret cults:

1). Members submit to an authoritarian, all-powerful leader, or leaders, whose decision cannot be questioned, and who discourage rational thought.
2). Members hold the opinion that the outside world is evil, and that cult and its members are "good" and the outside world is "bad or even" satanic.

3). Some groups are heavily armed and train their members to use weapons.

4). Cult leaders claim they need weapons because the outside world is against them.

5). Cults hold outside society and its laws and social moves in contempt because they believe their mission places them above human standards. They believe they have the truth and are working for the good of the world, or spiritual salvation, so their good justify even deceptive means.

For this paper therefore, "a cult is defined as being characterized by a total devotion, borne of conviction by a group of people to some ideal, practice, person, deity and rituals. It becomes secret when the members exclude non-members from participating (Ezeah, 2001).

Violence:

Oyedijo (1998), perceived violence as a state in which two parties are in opposition to each other. Also, it is a way of showing aggression and frustration among individuals and these individuals make up the community.

Highlighting the various forms of violence, Umo (2001) submits that it may be planned or unplanned, formal or spontaneous, verbal or physical, interpersonal or inter-group. It ranges from passive resistance to active aggression.

Obviously, cultism and violence are two inseparable threats to the peace and progress of any society. They pose serious treats and challenges to the administration of Nigerian higher institutions. Also, they instill a feeling of fear and repugnance in the society. Lives and property have been destroyed as a result of the rancorous cult members engaging themselves in uncontrolled self-indulgence acts. To stem the tide of human destruction, the society is obligated to curb these two contemptible and despicable social menaces. Believingly, adult counseling and education can be used as veritable tools to reduce the incessant incidences of cultism and violence in the Nigerian higher institutions in particular and in the society in general. This is the primary aim and objective of this chapter.

Origin of Cultism in Nigerian Institutions of Higher Learning:

According to Okirika (2001), the first recorded secret cult in the Nigerian educational institution started in 1953 at the former University College Ibadan. The secret cult at that time had "Pyrates Confraternity" as its popular cognomen founded by Professor Wole Soyinka. Ifeoma (2001) reported that this secret cult was legally registered under the corporate Affair Commission of Nigeria in 1976 as the National Association of Seadogs Pyrates Confraternity.

Pyrates Confraternity led by Professor Wole Soyinka was a remarkable protest against the prevailing injustices in the colonial public and educational administration. The initial aim of the cult was to foster African culture and ideologies, and also, to promote scholarship. Pyrates confraternity had a large follower because of its strong inclination to foster scholarship, which made it acceptable to the majority of its members. Pyrates confraternity's aims and objectives then spread to other parts of Nigerian institutions of higher learning. In this regard, cultism became more intensified and sophisticated, as many Nigerian institutions of higher learning became members.

The sudden upsurge of adolescents and young adults becoming involved in cultism led to the proliferations of secret cults in the Nigerian tertiary institutions. Ezeah (2001) submits that these cults bear blood-cuddling names and insignia like: The Mafia, Black Axe, the Pyrates, 'Eiye', the Maphites, Ku Klux Klan, the Viking Confraternity, Black Mamba, Mr. Lord, Sea Lord, Black Cat, the Buccaneers, Seadogs, the Black Devils, Black Belt, the Owl, Daughters of Jezebel, Amazons and Mgbagba, just to name a few.

Motives for Cult Membership:

Students join secret cults for various reasons. Wright (1994) highlights some of these reasons to include needs for recognition, protection and presumably power. Also, some students take to cultism as a mechanism of gaining mastery over intimidation from other students. Some go into cults just to boost their ego.

Udoffe (1991) and Odinakalu (1991) hold that cultism in Nigerian institutions of higher learning is an evident that confirms in the existence of secret cults in the larger society. Apparently, the larger society is permeated with cultism with the attendant evils of atrocity, acrimony, widespread moral decadence, maliciousness flagrancy and fraud. Regrettably, these evildoings have spread to the Nigerian institutions of higher learning worst than what is prevailing in the Nigerian larger society. For example, cultism in Nigerian institutions of higher learning is concomitant with violence, shooting, matcheting people to death, willful destruction of property, rape, hooliganism, arson and armed robbery. This is rather a regrettable phenomenon.

Incidences of Violent Secret Cult Activities in Institutions of Higher Learning in Nigeria:

The institutions of higher learning in Nigeria have witnessed numerous untoward incidences of cultic activities in the most recent times. This ugly situation has not only injected fear into the whole nation but also undermined the underlying pattern and structure of the institutions of higher learning in Nigeria. From every indication, cultism fosters belligerence among youths in the institutions of higher learning in Nigeria to the extent that it has now constituted a complicated and intractable issue in the Nigerian educational system.

For example, in 1991 tragedy struck as two fraternities, the Black Axe and 'Eiye' where in open and ferocious confrontation which resulted into the killing of a student at the University of Ibadan. The student was identified as a son of an army officer (Wright 1994). Also, the report of Vanguard 17th July 1999 has it that there was a grave upheaval in Lagos State University (LASU). Some members of secret cults in the institution collaborated with the cults members from the University of Lagos (UNILAG), and perpetrated a lethal and homicidal atrocity. They carried out their repugnant operation when the fresh students were matriculating. Four students were killed in the process. It was a tragic incident. Similarly, July 10th, 1999 was a mournful, gloomy and somber day at the Obafemi Awolowo University, Ile-Ife. The cult members besieged the residents of Awolowo and Fajuyi halls in the bloody operation which exterminated the lives of five students on that fateful day. Also, many students were lacerated. The great pandemonium that attended the dastardly acts truncated the academic program for the session. Of recent, July 2003 to be precise, some students of Polytechnic of Ibadan were arrested. They were indicted for possessing dangerous and sophisticated weapons on campus. They made their rebuttals that the weapons were meant to launch an invasive attack against another cults.

Obviously, these ugly incidents of cultism represent the prevailing scenario in most of the nation's institutions of higher learning, contended Ezeah (2001). It is on this note that some efforts have been geared towards weeding out the menace of cultism in the Nigerian institutions of higher learning.

Preferred Measures Against Cultism in Nigerian Institutions of Higher Learning

Obviously, the issue of cultism in the Nigerian institutions of higher learning has become a great concern in the society. It has therefore attracted the prompt attention of the governmental and non-governmental organizations. Also, many individuals, parents, guardians, relatives and friends of students in

Nigerian tertiary institutions have put forward numerous suggestions that can reduce the obnoxious cultic activities on campuses.

For example, it has been suggested that fresh students should be properly oriented to the adverse effects of cultism on campus. Such orientation should be comprehensive enough to educate the fresh students on the menace of cultism and the danger of being lured ignorantly into cultism. Okirika (2001) laments that what goes on these days as orientation for fresh students in some tertiary institutions is probably a one or two day talk to new students by renown scholars on a few academic areas. Such partial orientation is counter-productive.

It has equally been suggested that regular seminars and workshops on good human relationship and the dangers of cultism should be organized (Okirika, 2001). This measure to be effective should be complimented by moral instruction as a serious subject in the curriculum. The problem with this measure however, is that it treats the issue of cultism on the surface leaving the root untouched. Also, the students who are deeply involved in cultism may see the measure as imposition of idea which they may resist with utter aggression. This may aggravate the situation instead of helping it.

Moreover, it has been suggested that any discovered cult member apprehended should be rusticated. This measure sounds logical, effective and proportionate with the problem of cultism. However, experiences revealed that there had been considerable problems in enforcing it. For example, Olukoya (1997) cites the case of fifteen students of the University of Port Harcourt who were jailed in 1992 for fifteen years each for belonging to a campus cult. A Special Appeal Tribunal was set up, and the judgment was over-turned. Ezeah (2001) observes that where the school authority decides to hand over the students to the police, the parents of such cultists, who, in most cases are wealthy, secure their release before the case goes to court.

Other measures suggested to nip cultism in the bud include students organizing vigilante groups to arrest suspected cultists among themselves, overloading the students with all-inclusive and broad-spectrum of courses to occupy their time, cult education, dialogue between the government, parents students and school authorities and introduction of extra curricular activities like sports and different competitions.

Most of these measures have been taken. However, they are either abandoned or found ineffectual. This suggests that it is imperative to consider at this point another solution to curb the menace of cultism in the Nigerian institutions of higher learning.

The Roles of Adult Educators in the Eradication of Cultism and Violence

Traditionally, adult educators had been content experts restricted to literacy and post-literacy programs, but recently they are seen as playing numerous roles in all sectors of life (Onyemunwa, 1998). This new trend is based on the fact that the underpinning of the profession of adult education has been to foster and manage changes in the society. Hence, there is unprecedented and increased demand for adult and continuing education in every aspect of life. For example, the proliferation of tertiary institutions in Nigeria has been regarded as a welcome development. This has created an enlightened society where the vision for socio-cultural and economic development can become a reality. Many families can now boast of at least a graduate. Quite a few numbers of new tertiary institutions (mostly privately owned) have been established making the students population to rise. In this regard, there is need for the maximum participation of various governmental, non-governmental organizations, institution religious bodies and individuals to intervene in the proper management of the challenges, which the upsurge in population is posing. Obviously, cultism and violence in the institutions of higher learning in Nigeria remain the classical examples of such crises and challenges. Any effort geared towards curbing the menace of cultism and violence will not only bring sanity and peace into the academic atmosphere in the institutions of higher learning but will forestall incessant incidences of crimes in the society at large. This is because most of these cultists when they are rusticated or manage to graduate become terrors in the larger society.

One of the distinguishing features of a competent adult educator has been to identify real problems and through education seek ways to solve the problems. In this regard, the primary assignment of the adult educator is to facilitate the whole process of identifying the cause or causes of cultism and violence in the institutions of higher learning in Nigeria. One of the reasons why the problem of cultism with its concomitant effect of violence remains persistent is because the underpinning factors of cultism have not been properly identified. After the causes have been identified, enables the adult educators to identify the students involved in cultism and violence and counsel with them.

The adult educators can use their skill to design educational programs such as seminars, workshops or conferences to guide, stimulate and assist individual students involved in cultism and violence to desist from the obnoxious acts. Ofordile (2001) suggests that direct, non-threatening methods of educating parents, educators, police, counselors, and other professionals about this issue are needed. This underscores the role of adult educators to search for and involve the appropriate personnel who could lend valuable support in eradicating cultism and violence through education.

Conscientization is a household term in adult education. It means raising awareness or raising our consciousness. The adult educator has a vital role to play in this regard. Obviously, it may be difficult to find the lasting solution to the problem of secret cults in our institutions of higher learning in Nigeria forthwith. However, the adult educator by virtue of his professional expertise and creativity can be called upon to design educational programs that can raise the public awareness about the seriousness of the problem of in the higher institutions of learning.

Adult counselors and teachers are expected to understand the values and the prevailing norms and mores, which may influence students in tertiary institutions. In this respect the place of peer group and environmental factors are quite significant as well as their counseling needs. Okorodudu (1999) contends that positive interpersonal and human relationship among adults constitutes a major influence in helping adults to realize their educational goals and objectives. Similarly, interpersonal and human relation factors are very crucial or fundamental in helping the students in tertiary institutions. It is therefore the role of the adult educator as counselor and teacher to exploit and help to improve on the quality of interpersonal and human relationships among the students in tertiary institution to avert being lured into cults.

The issues of home background and parental influence are equally crucial in the whole process of eradicating cultism and violence in the institutions of higher learning. Adult educators must maintain a notable and high level of effective, cognitive, affective and instrumental relations with the students. This will enable them understand and appreciate the nature of home background and the influence acquired. Also, it would help the adult educators as counselors and teachers in selecting appropriate counseling theories such as Psychoanalytic theory of Sigmund Freud, Behavioral theory, Rational Emotive Therapy, for handling the cases of the students involved in cultism.

CONCLUSION

The obnoxious activities of cults in our institutions of higher learning have proved that something fundamental is wrong with the educational system in particular. The adult educators have their own roles to play in the whole process of alleviating the burden and menace of campus cults and violence in institutions of higher learning. And this has been the main thrust in this segment.

CHAPTER TWENTY-TWO

TEACHING STAFF PERFORMANCE, APPRAISAL, MOTIVATION, REWARDS AND PUNISHMENT

DR ADEYANJU 'LADE JOEL

INTRODUCTION

The wealth of a nation depends solely on the level of education of her people, and as often said, that no nation can rise above the level of her teachers, it becomes important to focus on the type and caliber of the teaching staff that man the educational institutions in Nigeria.

For over two decades, Nigerians have debated and have complained about the fall in Standards of Education. Decisions are very often passed on teacher's productivity and student's performance, when compared with the standards that was attained earlier on, in the 40s and about a decade after Nigeria's independence. The consensus as to whether there is a fall or not in educational standard in Nigeria is still an issue of controversy. A personal experience as a teaching staff in the Primary setting in the early 1970s seems to point to the facts that would— be teachers of the present generation needs serious attention, if they (teachers) would be able to assist the ever-rising population of learners within their control in present time. The section of the work attempts the topic: teaching staff performance, appraisal, motivation, rewards and punishment. Operational definitions will suffix thereafter, some of the factors that affect performance of teaching staff at the primary and secondary school levels will be addressed. The kinds of motivation that the teachers are given, and also the rewards expected, are considered important. Suggestions on suitable punishment would be provided. An attempt is made to examine who a teaching staff is, and the qualities of an effective teacher are also analyzed.

Teaching refers to a profession that was considered noble in the traditional past in Nigeria. Teachers provided instruction, gave advice to traditional chiefs, and taught Sunday school lessons, since most teachers were also catechists. As observed in the recent past, the teaching profession has been infiltrated by half-baked, untrained, and poorly trained teachers. To qualify as a trained teacher in the 40s, through late 60s, in Nigeria required a lot of rigorous academic work. The prospective teachers really have to sweat it out, and show the qualities of a disciplined personality. A trained teacher used to go through a five—year program in the teacher training college to qualify. He/she becomes a teaching staff after he/she has obtained a certificate. Teaching staff performance is therefore operationally defined as the ability of the teacher to carry out effectively his duties.

Motivation as defined by Hilgard, (1977) implies the regulation of need satisfying and goal seeking behavior. Morgan and king (1974) see motivation as the goal towards which behavior is directed. Since teachers are agents of change, they should set flexible goals to self-attainment, in order to avoid failure.

Eliot and Dweck (1983) observed that moderate goals expectations are better for the aspiring students, than far-fetched goals. Since teachers are placed in a position to assess performance of learners, it is important that reasonable goals are set.

Reward and Punishment as the psychologists put it refer to an equivalent of reinforcement in operant conditioning. Operant conditioning refers to efforts made at learning, to make a practical response to score positive reinforcement, or to avoid or escape painful stimulation, which is negative reinforcement. The learner would prefer to exhibit such behavior that would help him/her learn, than face an unpleasant situation, or a ridicule, or punishment.

Punishment on the other hand, refers to the application of an unpleasant stimulus, for the purpose of suppressing behavior that is negative.

It is a trained teacher that would make sufficient effort to bring about the required improvement in the learners. If we say that performance of children of the present day has fallen, it may be adduced to the nature of training that teachers of the mid 70s and 80s have received, and their un-committed attitude to work.

THE TRAINING OF TEACHERS

The government of Nigeria in the 70s, in her effort to increase the number of teachers, created the opportunity for a 'crash program.' This was done in order to execute the Universal Primary Education (UPE) scheme. It took two years to qualify as trained teachers then. It is still remembered that a pool of would—be teachers were secondary school certificate failures, and a large number among them found their way into the pivotal schools. Some of these crop of teachers never had any serious foundation as teachers, compared to those teachers that went through pupil teacher, Grade III, Grade 1, and then, qualify as elementary grade II certificate teachers.

An added problem of teachers performance transferred to fallen standard was the decision of the Federal government to close down most of the Grade II teacher training colleges in Nigeria. The aim was to set up colleges of education, but this effort has not been of much value. It is the same crop of school certificate holders that eventually moved into the colleges of education, as many of them, cannot get to any university. In which case, the intrinsic interest of becoming a teacher has never been there, (Adeyanju 1995).

It is unfortunate to state that the Federal Government Teachers Training College at Toro, in the former Benue Plateau State in Nigeria, now in Bauchi State, was the second oldest training college in the whole of Northern Nigeria, the first being Katsina Teachers College, which was opened in 1927, and presently, its status has been changed to that of a secondary school.

Since teachers no longer go through the hitherto rigorous requisite rudimentary training of professionals, there is bound to be mass production of poor teaching staff, and this in turn, affects the performance of the students. The qualities that make up an effective and efficient teacher are discussed hereafter.

TEACHERS' QUALITIES

A teacher would normally instruct learners, using appropriate methodology to transport his ideas, knowledge and facts to them. A teacher takes cognizance of individual differences, and provides necessary attention for them. A teacher prepares his lesson ahead of time, what he wants to teach. He teaches using necessary instructional materials and aids. Marking of assignments and attending to learners needs is a priority. He teaches learners through encouragement and motivation. He gives rewards, in terms of praises (appreciation), for example, by clapping of hands, and also punishes poor behavior. An effective teacher should be smart, neatly dress, cautious and well comported. The teacher is a leader. He gives respect accordingly to those he teaches, and the colleagues he/she interacts with in school. A trained teacher should be friendly, firm and should be seen as a man/woman of good reputation. He/she should be disciplined, and should display very good mastery of his subject teaching, and related areas.

It may be wise to attempt an appraisal of the teachers that are in the primary, secondary and tertiary institutions. In order to do justice to teacher performance appraisal, he/she has several tasks (duties) with a common denominator; he/she (teacher) is a master and a guide to learners.

Teacher's personalities have been studied, and found to be a significant factor in successful teaching. The statistical procedure of Ryan and Beechers, summarized the instrument that has been used to evaluate teachers effectiveness. Bush researched intensively at nearly every facet of the relationship between teacher and student, and found that mutual liking of teacher and pupil occurred in only 15 per cent of the cases, and that a teacher's liking for student appears to be unrelated to competence.

In order to appraise the teachers' personality, it may be of help to screen them for the following:

1. Is the teacher a good representative of our culture, with self-respect for self, and others; does he behave a free person in a free study?
2. Is he/she intelligent enough to think with power and able to stimulate most of his best students to behave in like manners?
3. Is he/she emotionally controlled, flexible as situation demands, drive steadily toward self-imposed goals, maintain balance and recover quickly in difficult situations.
4. Is he/she exceptionally healthy, imaginative with special aptitudes a well round person of many wide interests, capable of reading widely in different fields?
5. Does he/she like people and can work with them without being emotionally dependent on them? A teacher is expected to portray the above traits, in addition to having a strong conviction of the power of education, and teachers' worth to society. Using some or all of the above, the teacher can self evaluate the self, and make adjustment.

APPRAISAL OF THE TEACHERS' ABILITY, INTELLIGENCE AND PROBLEMS

In traditional times, teachers' responsibility in the elementary and secondary schools revolved around drilling students to remember facts, and formula's (mastery of time table, date in the month and year, memorizing facts and committing to memory the geographical features of the world at large; and master of the 'student companion' a bible for the current and documented events. The focus on question of intelligence was therefore largely conjectural.

Advance in science and technology has turned the whole world into a global village, a window through which increasing complexity of knowledge and living about the seen and unseen world has to be mastered by the present day teacher in order for him/her to function. These are serious challenges, and teachers of today should be people of considerable natural endowment.

The contemporary teacher should be knowledgeable about contributions of men and times to the development of society. He/She should be able to discuss important issues now confronting mankind. He/she should master his special field, and should be able to relate with closely allied fields. He/She should master how children grow and develop, and have to adapt, inspire and impart knowledge to growth levels. He should know how students learn and how to improve desirable outcomes or results. He/she should be able to communicate effectively in language of the immediate environment, and in English. It is also expected that he possesses the ability and application of the research of others. The ability to unify all his knowledge into a meaningful philosophy is very important.

The appraisal of teaching staff performance implies that the teacher's personality, his special abilities, his knowledge and intelligence, are important.

As mentioned earlier, the kind of teaching that goes on in the primary and secondary schools in Nigeria as exhibited by teachers leaves more to be desired, and this is a result of lack of interest. In fact this problem cuts across all the 6-3-3-4 system of the Nigeria educational system. The circumstances that may have led to this situation may be the neglect, and the lack of the federal governments' interest to provide adequate funding. It is also considered that the assumption that anybody can be a teacher, is counter productive to the profession, such that teaching can be the choice of the unemployed, and virtually in any field, and this choice is also often made as a last resort.

The popular opinion is that going through the National Certificate of Education (NCE) is enough to qualify one to be an effective teacher. This is a wrong assumption.

Similarly, the Federal Government of Nigeria has tried to make it compulsory for teachers at the primary school to qualify as NCE holders by the year 2000. This step has also failed. The unequal response to issues of the development of education between the North and South is a big problem, since the North is still fairly backward in her educational pursuits.

While many more people have rushed into upgrading their teaching skills, a large percent have no deep interest in teaching, other than for the purpose of keeping their jobs. Meanwhile, the National Teachers Institute in Kaduna, has taken over the training of teachers completely, and now offers the training on a weekend basis. The problem is that part-time teaching is given to thousands of Nigerians would be teachers on a weekend basis. Another problem is that teachers are still poorly remunerated, and there is delay in payment of their salaries. There is also the Federal and State governments' insensitivity to the plight of teachers. From the different states that make up the federation, arbitrary deductions are made from the monthly allocations to the Teaching Service Commissions. Incentives are diverted elsewhere, and agreements reached with the government most of the times, somehow are not fulfilled. This action has contributed to 'brain drain'. Under the present circumstances, the 'best' of teachers is no longer given to learners. Teachers appear rather tired, and this is in a way, is an indicator of the fall in standard of education in the country. Who is to blame? The Federal government has continued to encourage the opening of more private schools, colleges, and Universities. These steps the government may lead, albeit unwittingly, to other serious problems, including giving poor quality education to the Nigerian populace, because of possible appointment of poor teaching staff, with a view to maximizing their profit.

TEACHERS ROLE IN SCHOOLING

Teachers perform significant roles in the society and community to which they belong. They occupy a peculiar position in the family they belong, and are role models in religious circles. They show the light and the way.

In Havighurst (1981) view, teachers are public servants; they are surrogate of middle class minority, experts and leaders in different areas of the community, and agents of social change.

Teachers are charged with educating learners, so that they have all round development as persons that are morally, intellectually, spiritually, emotionally and physically sound. The teacher therefore becomes the custodian of ideals and values that the society expects the children to learn in school. The teacher's performance in his/her expected role forms a subject of debate in present times. The issue at stake revolves around the need for teachers to improve performance of their roles as:

(1) Mediator of learning, (ii) Disciplinarian and controller of student behavior, (iii) Parent substitute, (iv) judge of learner's achievement (vi) Organizer of the curriculum, (vii) as bureaucrat, (viii) as scholar and Research specialist and (ix) as members contributing positively to teachers organization.

An appraisal of the first three roles viz: mediator of learning, disciplinarian and controller of student behavior, as experienced among the present generations of teachers inform us that performance in these areas is extremely poor. The attention of a number of young teachers is directed at 'making it' fast. This is the case in present day Nigeria. The resultant effect is what we see in examination malpractices, collusion with the bad eggs to defraud the system, and abject indiscipline.

The next three roles and performance of teachers as observed in present time is equally questionable. Is the teacher a good confidant to students any more? Teachers take gifts in kind as reward from their students. This act is immoral.

Some teachers move dangerously too close with their students.

This act sometimes leads to putting the girl child in family way. It is also sad to say that only few teachers may be sincere judges of learners' achievements, which shouldn't be, no matter the pressure.

Teachers are supposed to be better organizers of the curriculum. The problem is that the teachers teaching interest may not be there, and when teachers fail to prepare the lesson they ought to teach, how will the content be taught? The teaching is likely to be very poor.

From a recent sample opinion of teachers, and undergraduate students in the field on teaching practice assignment, the issue of teaching has not been taken as a serious matter. If teachers will fail to research and read more on aspects of the lesson to teach, the measure of performance would be questionable. As regards teachers' contribution to teacher organization, it appears that only the Nigeria Union of Teachers (NUT) leadership makes some impact, if any. At the local level, teachers organize lessons for the upper classes; teachers prepare their students for the popular school certificate examination, National Examinations Council (NECO) and the Joint Admission and Matriculation Board (JAMB). These steps are partly taken because of the financial benefits derivable from it. The Parent Teachers Association (PTA) of schools has come up to assist by employing and paying teachers, where such specialist teachers are not available in secondary schools. Who is to blame and what factors have led to the observed degeneration of the teaching staff performance?

What the teacher does to motivate learners?

Hirst and Peters (1970) argued that interest in teaching has more relevance to the methods of teaching than to its content. No teacher would want poor results, this is why the effective teachers spend more time preparing what to teach and how to teach it, and he/she often ask the self the questions that he/she wish to ask learners. Teachers who are able to take some time preparing seriously to teach are considered better motivators of interest of pupils. Are teachers of present day not considering teaching too burdensome? Who will do extra job of teaching without getting paid for it? If teachers are to perform creditably well, they all need to be motivated as well.

MOTIVATION OF TEACHERS

Apart from ensuring that teacher's salaries are paid on time and as at when due, several other benefits should be worked out for them.

The 'best teachers award exercise' should be instituted in all the thirty-six states of the federation of Nigeria. This is the practice in Ghana. Teachers should also organize themselves for remedial teaching program. Opportunity to educate the self further, with financial support from both the government and private sector should be made available to help teachers.

It is necessary to challenge the Nigeria Union of Teachers (NUT) leadership in Nigeria. This body should create commercial ventures with the money they keep in the cooperative organization. Such money can be reinvested in the construction of 'Teachers hostels', which lodgers can use at reduced rates, as found in Teachers Hostels in Ghana. It is no news that teachers cannot boast of owning their personal houses on retirement.

CONCLUSION AND Recommendation

Teachers should be encouraged to study and write in their own fields. The appraisal of teacher's performance should take cognizance of the ability of the English teachers' creative writing. Teachers should publish stories for children at the elementary school level, and performance by students, should be assessed on a cumulative record basis.

According to Bush studies, students like teachers whom they regard as high in knowledge of subject. Pupils tend to like teachers that could inspire their liking the subject matter achievement. In order to improve performance of teachers,

teachers that view their teaching experience with inadequacies of background should be given opportunity for training and retraining. This proposition will enable the teacher know about his field and teaching success.

Issues concerning teaching staff performance, motivation, reward and punishment have been appraised. As it is often asserted, if the pupils have not learned, then the teacher has not taught. As concerned citizens, we need to work hard to salvage the image of the Teaching profession. While the committed teachers' may be working very tirelessly at improving standard, it is considered that without giving them the necessary incentives, and without finding a lasting solution to indiscipline in our society, worthwhile standard will become unattainable.

CHAPTER TWENTY-THREE

IMPACT OF GENDER INEQUITY AND INEQUALITY OF INCOME DISTRIBUTION ON AFRICA'S DEVELOPMENT DRIVE

PROFESSOR JANET OLUSI

INTRODUCTION

The consideration of gender roles in economic development is somehow recent. It can be traced to the implementation of policies designed to achieve fundamental transformation in the economics of Asia, Latin America and Africa. Such countries have experienced serious economic recessions, and hence have had to implement a package of stabilization and adjustment strategies recommended by the World Bank (IBRD) and International Monetary Fund (IMF). Such adjustment packages often referred to as Structural Adjustment Programs (SAP) aim at getting factor and product prices right to make them reflect their true economic costs in such countries.

In trying to achieve this objective, it became quite clear that gender roles in production, need to be considered generally in national economics and particularly at the household levels. Thus, the usual assumption of homogeneity of factors, particularly labor and equality of opportunities, which often reflected in development programs, has to be reconsidered. It is becoming more realistic to augment macro development policies, with such policies, which focus on gender contributions to development. In that process, problems of poverty, inequity and the resulting inequality of income distribution are receiving greater focus than pre-SAP. Adjustment Strategies need to embrace measures to empower the poor to make an economically efficient contribution to development. Furthermore, there is the recognition of gender inequality as a significant subset of general inequality in income distribution and the realization that women who constitute a high proportion of population in such countries represent the bulk of the poor. Although the implementation of SAP recommendations has drawn attention to differences in gender roles, it has not changed the relationship. For most countries, SAP has worsened female opportunities (Palmer, 1991), and hence there is need to look for more fundamental causes of gender inequity and propound appropriate solutions for them. This is because inequality of income distribution has been recognized as a major cause of low rates of economic development (Todaro, 1985). By drawing examples from Africa in general and Nigeria is particular, this paper highlights economic relationships which are responsible for gender inequality exhibited in access to income generating opportunities and the resultant inequality of income distribution patterns usually skewed against women in developing countries.

Specifically, this chapter:

(a) Examines theoretical assertions on income distribution.

(b) Highlights gender patterns of income distribution in African countries viz-a-viz the developed ones.

(c) Advances reasons for gender inequality and inequality of income distribution and relates this to the level and pace of economic development in 3rd world countries.

(d) Isolates efforts being made to close the gap and

(e) Assesses the adequacy of such efforts and makes suggestions for improvement.

a.   Theoretical Assertions on Income Distribution

Basic economics recognizes an economic system as consisting of two groups of actors namely the business firms and the household. These participate in the markets for goods and services flow from business firms to households who make payments for them in form of money. On the other hand, households supply labor and capital to business firms and receive payments in forms of rents, wages, salaries, dividends, interest, (Leftwich, 1973). On individual basis, the income earned depends on (a) the quantities of different resources that he can put into the production process and (b) the price he receives for them.

Thus an individual who owns just his labor power will have his total income determined by the wage rate and the total time period he works for. However, an individual who owns land and has some capital resources will in addition to his wages earn rent and interest. Income distribution is therefore a function from large quantities of resources owned and properly placed in employments where they contribute much to consumer satisfaction. Income differences then arise from two sources namely; (i) improper channeling of resources to productive process and (ii) from differences in resources ownership among individuals. While the former tends to be self-correcting, through mobility of factors to their different alternative uses, the latter, that is resources ownership distortions are not self-correcting. The self correcting mechanism of income differences may however be delayed by ignorance on the part of factors such as labor or factor owners or by institutional barriers that prevent factor mobility.

The major sources of differences in resources ownership include differences in labor power owned (e.g. differences in physical and mental inheritance and opportunities some types of training). Differences in capital owned in kind and quality arise from initial differences in labor resources owned and difference in material inheritance, fortuitous circumstances such as chance, luck, fraud and individual propensities to accumulate.

The above analysis of causes and sources of differences in income distribution will go along with differences in natural resources endowment and technological know-how to explain differences in income among countries of the world. The degree of inequality of income distribution varies from one country to another but they are more pronounced in the 3rd world countries where it has been proved that the poorest 20 percent of population receive less than 5 percent of total national incomes while the highest 10 percent receive about 40 percent of income (Todaro 1985). By contrast, developed countries have exhibited more equal distribution of incomes because they have been able to develop over the years the necessary effective mechanisms to transfer some production of incomes from the rich to the poor. Such methods include the alternation of fundamental distribution of income through policies designed to change relative factor price and modifying the personal or size distribution of income through progressive asset ownership redistribution.

The foregoing considerations of income inequality by traditional economics have not discussed gender differences. Even though they constantly refer to households and the business firms, there is the underlying assumption that households consist of homogenous units. Although traditional economics recognizes the existence of poverty arising from inequity and inequality of income distribution, it fails to uphold the emerging facts that the female gender faces considerable discrimination in this distribution. A more realistic approach to the study of the causes and sources of poverty in 3rd world countries will of necessity use the foregoing economic analyses to expose the disadvantaged position of the female gender in income distribution and this is done in the next section.

b.   Gender Analysis if income Determinants in Africa.

The major determinants of income as analyzed above are employment status and resources ownership patterns among individuals. A gender analysis of these in African Countries vis a vis the developed countries of the world gives a clearer view of the economic problems of the continent.

A breakdown of female employment status in the continent shows that of African women as compared with their counterparts in the developed countries, (see table 1) has a downward trend.

Table 1:   Employment Status of Female Labor Force (1990–1992) Females Share of Labor Force (Percent)

COUNTRY	1970	1972
Mozambique	50	47
Sierra Leone	36	32
Malawi	45	41
Kenya	42	39
Nigeria	37	34
Togo	39	36
Ghana	42	40
Zimbabwe	38	34
Cote D'Ivoire	38	34
Cameroon	37	33
Morocco	1	21
South Africa	33	36
Botswana	44	35
Ireland	26	29
United Kingdom	36	39
Canada	32	40

United States	37	41
Switzerland	33	36

Sources: (i)   The World Bank Human Development Reports, 1990: Oxford
University Press.

(ii)   The World Bank World Development Report, 1994: Oxford
University Press.

This data typically represents workers in the public and private formal sector service but often exclude women in the informal sectors. The falling share of women labor in Africa and the increasing share of men's suggests that more men earn wages than women. Since wages constitute a major subset of total individual income, this to a large extent explains gender inequality of income distribution. Lower employment of females in the public and private formal sectors in Africa may be due to lower formal education and higher illiteracy status of women in the continent (see table 2).

Table 2:   Education and Illiteracy Status of Females in Selected African Countries

COUNTRY	FEMALE PER 100 MALES				ADULT LITERACY %	
	Primary		Secondary			
	1990	1991	1990	1991	Female	Total
Sierra Leone	67	70	40	56	89	79
Malawi	59	82	36	53	*	*
Nigeria	59	76	49	74	61	49
Ghana	75	82	35	63	49	40
Cote D'Ivoire	57	71	27	47	60	46
Cameroon	74	85	36	71	57	46
Mali	55	58	99	50	76	68
Togo	45	65	86	34	69	57
Kenya	71	95	42	78	42	31
Zimbabwe	79	99	63	88	40	33
Uganda	65	*	31	*	65	53

* figures not available

Source: World Bank World Development Report, 1994, Oxford University
Press.

The figures show that for most countries, the number of female percentage, relative to male, declines as levels of education increase from primary through secondary education. This implies, lower skill, and hence lower employment level, and the ultimate income accruing to women in such countries. Lower employment of women may however be due to institutional factors like religious and cultural barriers, which may prevent women from taking up appointments in the formal sectors. There also exist problems of inequity such as discrimination against women in granting them access to relevant training for some posts in the public and formal business sectors. For instance, Ijere (1991) recorded that school curriculum in Nigeria for a long time was geared to reflect the role assigned to women, which is mainly home management for rearing children. Hence most women ended up in the teaching and nursing profession in the early stages of western education in Nigeria. On the other hand men were exposed to courses in science to prepare them for more vigorous professions like engineering and medicine.

Sometimes, discrimination against female labor arises because of employers' unwillingness to pay wages during maternity leaves and their belief that labor is not homogenous and females are less efficient than their male counterparts even when exposed to the same type of training. Also, labor immobility affects female labor that males and hence, well-qualified female workers may be reluctant to take up appointments, since they have to take care of their homes.

It is pertinent to mention that it is in the agricultural sector, which is the mainstay of most African economies that the greatest gender biases occur (Palmer, 1991). Many writers (Baserup, 1970; Due, 1986; Witchterich, 1985; Ijere, 1991; Galdwin, 1991) have confirmed that women perform more than 60 percent of agricultural work yet monetary rewards and the relations of production in the sector are skewed against them in Africa. The main explanation for this is the non-monetisation of their economic activities in agriculture as food produced is mainly for subsistence while cash incomes from their husbands' farms where they (the women) also render services accrue to the men who are often reluctant to make such available for their families' needs. Thus, intra houschold distribution of budget control, does not favor women. This trend in income has become more pronounced since SAP because of the commercialization of hitherto non-commercial food crops often referred to as "women crops". Male farmers have switched their resources to the production of women crops as soon as they become commercialized (Mkandawire, 1989) thereby further marginalizing women from their traditional productive earnings. This leads to the consideration of the second major determinant of income, which is:

Resources Ownership

The pattern of resources ownership in Africa favors the male gender. This is because inheritance practices are mainly patriarchal which absolves women from inheriting key resources like land needed for farming, commercial buildings and other capital assets. The land, which they farm are usually temporarily given to them by their fathers, husbands or are mainly leaseholds hence they have no rights of ownership (Adekanye, 1993). Moreover, such lands are often close to their homes and productivity is minimal. Extension services, such as the use of capital inputs, often provided by government, focus attention on men, because change agents are men. Hence, the distribution of traditional farming development resources is also skewed against women (Adekanye et al, 1995). This factor widens the gap in income between males and females. As regards off-farm incomes, women engage mainly in petty trading and are rarely known to be large-scale producers or foremost entrepreneurs. This is largely due to their limited investible funds and their little consideration is the advancement of loanable funds by financial houses. This is as a result of the usual reason of women's inability to supply the relevant collaterals in forms of land and other necessary assets.

Another set of determinants of income as recognized in Economics literature are such fortuitous circumstances like luck, chance, fraud. Experience has shown that such circumstances are common among public office holders and since women are poorly represented in the decision making echelon in African countries (see Table 3), only a small proportion can make incomes from such resources. Moreover, women have lower propensity to accumulate wealth than men since studies have shown that they spend their extra incomes on providing basic necessities for their families (Kennedy, 1989; Bouis and Haddad, 1990; Braun and Kennedy, 1986).

Table 3:   <u>**Distribution of Some Key Posts in Nigeria in 1992**</u>

POST	TOTAL	MALE	FEMALE
Federal Director-General	22	20	02
Ministries	29	29	00
Governors	30	30	00
State Assembly	1,172	1,145	27
Judges of the High Court	13	13	00

Source: Computed from Nigerian Yearbook, 1992

The foregoing discussion highlights major causes of gender inequity and inequality of income distribution in developing countries typified by the African situation. This obviously slows down the rate of development in such countries hence it is necessary to see the effects of this gender inequality and uneven distribution of income in such countries as done in the next section.

c.   **Effects of Gender Inequality and Inequality of Income Distribution on 3rd World Countries**

According to Adam Smith (1976), "No society can surely be flourishing and happy of which by far the greater part of the numbers are poor and miserable". Although gender inequality and its resultant inequality of income distribution is a small part of the broader problems of inequality in developing countries (others being inequality of prestige, status, recognition, job satisfaction and freedom of choice), its effects cannot be overlooked. In most cases, income inequality and poverty are more apparent than other forms of inequity. Also, given the high proportion of females in the population of 3rd world countries, there is a way in which the effects of gender income inequality represents all forms of poverty in such countries.

The first effect of inequality is seen in the production and consumption patterns in the countries. Such patterns are dictated by the preferences of the few rich who are most likely to be men given the conditions for earning higher incomes discussed earlier in this paper. This is probably the reason why basic needs like food are scarce. Nigeria for instance, imports most of her cereals when in reality most of her women population (about 80%) live in the rural areas and work on food crop farms (Ijere, 1991). Gender inequity and income inequality therefore worsen the problems of low productivity and food production in 3rd world countries.

On the macro level, gender inequality and inequality of income worsens the problem of poverty of 3rd world countries vis-à-vis the developed ones. Low productivity, female labor unemployment and under development which are rampant in such countries have an overall multiplier effect of lowering the growth rate of national and per capital products which are standard economic measures of poverty.

High population growth rates have been recorded in third world countries. A major cause often advanced for this is early female marriages resulting from gender inequity and therefore causing gender inequality of income distribution and the poverty of nations.

Perhaps the most serious implications of gender inequality of income distribution is manifested in the management of households and the low levels
of living of rural sectors who constitute the highest proportion of third world
countries. Because women's incomes are relatively low, they cannot perform
their roles of providing basic needs of food and good nutrition for their household hence the prevalence of high infant mortality rates vis-à-vis those of
developed countries (See table 4).

Table 4:   Health and Nutrition in Selected Developing and Developed
            Countries

COUNTRIES	LOW BIRTH WEIGHT BABIES (%) 1990	INFANT MORTALITY RATE (PER 100) LIVE BIRTHS		PREVALENCE OF MALNUTRITION UNDER 5 (1987–1992)
		1970	1992	
Mozambique	20	156	162	*
Tanzania	14	132	92	25.2
Sierra Leone	17	197	143	*
Malawi	20	193	134	*
Nigeria	15	139	84	35.7
Ghana	17	111	81	27.1
Cote D'lvore	14	135	91	12.4
Morocco	9	128	57	11.8
Botswana	8	101	35	15.0
United Kingdom	7	19	7	*
United State	7	20	9	-
Switzerland	5	15	6	-

Source: World Bank, World Development Report 1994, Oxford University
           Press.

The table shows very high infant mortality rates in developing countries and
low rates in developed ones thereby supporting the view that health standards
are very poor in 3rd world countries. This is obviously the negative impact of
gender inequity in developing countries. The pertinent question of hope for
improvement in these countries can be considered within the framework of

what they are doing to bridge the gap in gender equality and the adequacy of such efforts. This is done in the next section.

V. Efforts to Close the Gap in Gender Inequity and Inequality of Income Distribution and their Adequacy for the Situations of 3rd World Countries

Gender poverty arises from gender inequity that is so obvious in 3rd world countries. Attempts at closing the gap can be considered from two points of view namely (i) government policies and (ii) activities of non-governmental organizations.

In Nigeria, government policies have been directed at introducing new production technologies to women and making available to them the financial and land resources necessary for adopting such technologies. The most recent of such policies are the Better Life for rural women program initiated by the former first Lady, Mrs. Mariam Babangida and operated from 1987 to 1992. This has now been replaced by another like it but which claims to be gender neutral by focusing attention on the family and tagged "Family support program" initiated by Mariam Abacha the present first lady. Apart from introducing new production technologies, the programs have other components like the promotion of women's education, provision of social and health facilities and facilities and reducing women's child caring burden by providing child daycare facilities. Popular as these programs have been in recent times, their effects are seriously limited by two factors. In the first place, the ability of women to enjoy these facilities depends on their membership of cooperative societies when are duty registered with the programs. Most cooperative societies could not get registered with the Better Life Program and hence their members could not enjoy the production facilities provided under the program. This factor of non-involvement of most women also implies low cover age for such programs and hence minimal impact on gender equity.

Efforts made by local non-governmental organizations that have organizations that have permeated most countries in form of cooperative societies are also directed at alleviating women's poverty. In Nigeria, local NGO's like the Country Women's Association (COWAN) and Community Women Development (COWAD) are well known. By sourcing funds from International organizations to augment personal efforts, these associations make credit and relevant resources including training available to their members to enable them undertake economic activities. However, the achievements of such organizations are often limited by scarcity of funds.

A third group of associations that have become interested in gender in-equity and are committed to minimizing it are the International Non-governmental Organizations like UNICEF and UNDP, UNICEF in Nigeria got involved in agricultural production by providing improved cassava cuttings, soybeans, maize, groundnut, rice and bean seed to women for planting in some parts of Nigeria (The Guardian, Feb. 5, 1992). Obviously, Such activities will enhance women's productivity and their ultimate incomes. The UNDP is much more interested in the control of the environment and this means a lot of help to women since they interact more with the environment than men (Adakanye, 1993; Awe 1993). However direct help rendered by International organizations to alleviate the poverty of women specifically are still in their infancy and so their impacts cannot be assessed objectively yet.

Even though the achievements of government policies on gender equity are minimal, the awareness of the adverse effects of this phenomena and the need to reduce it creates hope for the future. Reporting on ILO's activities, Christian Oppng (1992) reported that more women in Africa than before now partici-pate in informal sector works, which suggests that they are no wage earners as against their former un-commoditized functions within their households. In trying to balance access to educational facilities and training there are rays of hope for many 3rd world countries. Apart from the fact that female enrolment in primary schools are sometimes higher than that of their male counterparts, there are significant improvements in female enrolment in higher institutions. The Nigerian University enrolment, as shown in table 5, supports this fact. This suggests higher skills for women and greater efficiency in the process of production.

Table 5:   Total Enrolment in Nigerian Universities by Sex 1985–1990

YEAR	TOTAL M & F	FEMALE	FEMALE % OF TOTAL
1995/86	107,204	25,067	31.0
1986/87	120,753	29,397	32.0
1987/88	130,548	33,229	34.0
1988/89	141,219	37,456	36.0
1989/90	147,145	39,218	36.0

Source: Federal Ministry of Education, Statistics of Education in Nigeria, 1985–1989 (1990 edition)

The table shows a consistent increase in female percentage of total enroll-ments in the Nigerian Universities.

Even in the agricultural sector, women are gradually protesting their non-monetized roles. For instance Palmer (1991) quoted Joeke et al (1988), that Mali women refused to grind the increase in men's maize output because they saw no monetary return even when they had to give up some self provisioning work to do it. Pockets of this type of protests are becoming aware of their rights and are claiming them.

The foregoing discussion of what are being done to close the gap in gender inequity and inequality in income distribution can be seen as mainly having long term effects on gender relationships. Developing countries need to apply strategies that will work both in the short, the medium and the long terms if gender inequity is to be reduced. The consideration of such strategies are hence analyzed in the next section.

VI. Policy Suggestions

Public policies are more effective in removing gender biases in the short term because innovations designed to improve women's access to public resources such as working capital and technical information can be achieved through legal reforms. Feasible solutions to inequity can be achieved by directing financial institutions to give women a better chance in granting credit. The Nigerian people's banks have this as one of their objectives but the practicability of this factor is yet to be ascertained.

In line with the suggestions of theoretical economics, a redistribution of income by gender can be achieved by taxing sales of men's produce and using the proceeds to finance investments in women's higher labor productivity. In order to ensure that more women receive formal education, quotes could be used to favor female entrants while there could be discrimination against males in payments for education and health facilities. Governments can also legislate in support of employment of more women in the informal sector.

For long-term solution, education and training facilities should be designed to prepare boys and girls equally for production practices. This will remove the fear of employers as regards the homogeneity of labor. This will also ensure adequate preparation of women for self-employment thus making them entrepreneurs like men.

The removal of inequity in agriculture requires more fundamental changes than human resources development. It requires the assurance of higher productivity for women in that sector through their assured control of the resources they manage. This point, which has already been discussed as a constraint may be difficult to achieve in African countries because such resources control by women will be seen as impinging on men's authority over them (women). Land reforms may not succeed. Nigeria's land use Decree of 1978 has failed to secure land for end users who are not original owners, it might be more difficult then to use decrees to secure land resources for women. Efforts can however be directed at making women's tenancy of certain assets they manage more permanent for instance, land given to a women to farm by her husband should be left for her to continue to manage even if she becomes a widow.

Lastly, women's domestic unremunerated labor services constitute a constraint on their achievement of gender equity. The provision of social goods such as pipe-borne water and electricity will relieve women of their reproductive duties and enable them take up employment for wages. Also, the provision of official child minding centers during working hours will give more time to women to work in the public and informal sectors. It might be argued economically that this will imply higher government expenditure, such can infant be financed by taxing men more highly to finance the programs. A combination of these measures will reduce gender inequity and narrow down the gap income distribution while the quality of life that is so much dependent on women's economic activities will improve considerably in 3rd world countries.

CHAPTER TWENTY-FOUR

FEMALE-LABOR IMMOBILITY AS CONSTRAINT ON WELFARE INCREASE

PROFESSOR JANET OLUSI

INTRODUCTION

The last two decades have witnessed global attention on women's activities, and their invaluable roles, in the effort to achieve economic development, particularly in low income countries. Generally, there is an agreement among writers and observers of world economy that women represent the bulk of the poor all over the world. Mary Evans (1994) confirms that women constitute half of the world's population, they do three-quarters of the world's work, earn 10% of the world income and own 1% of the world's property. The most recent United Nations Organizations publication on the role of women in development (The World's Women, 1994) confirms this position of women. It states that 60% of the world's rural population, consisting of 550 million women, live below poverty line. While this is said to represent 50 percent increase for women, only 30 percent more of men live below poverty line, since the 1970's. Since women represent about half of the world's population, their poverty condition poses a great challenge to development, and as put by the UNO report (1994), "It represents a major failure of development".

The manifestation of poverty varies among nations of the world, within countries, and at the intra household level, where poor consumption patterns are indicators of its presence. There is a general agreement however, that the developing countries of Asia, Latin America and Sub-Saharan Africa posses ad manifest greater features of poverty (UNO, 1994).

It is also true that efforts to alleviate poverty in such countries are frustrated by socio-cultural and economic factors, which are skewed against women. It is important to note however that in spite of the recognition of women's poverty, and their potential roles in development, as better home managers (Kennedy, 1987; Haddad, 1991), the constraint against their full participation have not been fully identified, nor have specific policies and action programs been adequately developed for achieving this goal (Mueller and Ankar, 1990), suggestions such as increasing women's access to land, (Olusi, 1995; Adekanye, 1993), credit and better participation in decision making (Olusi 1995) have however been made. Others include the introduction of appropriate technology, health services, and good housing schemes to women.

Writers from both developed and Third world countries have emphasized women's low level of employment as a strong reason for their poverty. The non-monetization of women's household work has also been stressed (Olusi, 1995; Folbre 1995). An area that has not received much emphasis is female labor immobility, as a cause of poverty, and as a major cause of their low participation in development. The issue of female labor immobility as a strong constraint on welfare increase is the main focus of this section. Hence the chapter examines:

(a) The work situation of women in Nigeria.
(b) Mobility concept and causes of gender differentials in labor mobility within the formal and informal sectors of Nigeria as proxy for most developing countries.
(c) The effects of these differentials on welfare and makes suggestions.

Section 2: Women's Participation in the Labor Force, an Overview.

Both the ILO publication (Oppong 1992) and UNO (1994) claim that when considered globally, more women now go out to work as paid labor than in the 70's and before. Globally, UNO reports that about 854 million women were economically active in 1990, accounting for 32. 1% of the global labor force. However there are conspicuous regional differences, indicating the range of socio-economic status and women's emancipation ratio of between 33 and 44 percent. African countries have low participation rates, and Nigeria in particular recorded about 25.45 percent. This suggests that about ¾ of women workers in the country do not earn wages. A usual explanation for this low participation for women in Africa in general and Nigeria in particular is the adoption of Structural Adjustment Programs (SAP) in the 1980's. In Nigeria, SAP was adopted without any options and such policies required freedom to trade internationally in hitherto restricted goods, reduction of parastatals, funding by governments, deregulation of foreign exchange, and the removal of oil subsidy, in the case of Nigeria. These policies have been particularly detrimental to female labor force participation in the continent (Gladwin 1991, Elson 1991, Palmer 1991). For instance, reduction of parastatal funding led to reduction of workers, and women were mostly affected by such retrenchment, since they were employed mainly as temporary workers, or as low cadre workers, and hence, became vulnerable to retrenchment occasioned by SAP.

In general, female representation in the wage-earning sector is very poor in Nigeria because of the prevailing belief that the primary role of a woman is domestic, that is care rendering as wife and mother. Hence, majority of women are not prepared by the educational system for better jobs beyond service rendering occupation, such as teaching, and nursing, among others, (Ijere 1991). Moreover, women are rarely trained to provide for their own economic security (Aina, 195). The decline in public sector employment restrict women's bargaining power in the labor market, hence, their immobility and low contribution to welfare (UNO, 1994). In the industries, women are recruited into the more casual forms of labor. In Nigeria, they are concentrated in a few occupations termed "women jobs," and such are extensions of their domestic roles. Table 1 confirms this.

Employment in the Administrative and other services section is not much different, when analyzed by gender as shown below.

The foregoing discussions confirm that women's representation in government establishments is low. Also, women employed in such establishments face subtle discriminations. Until quite recently in Nigeria, women's leave bonuses were much less than those of their male counterparts on the same salary grade (Makinwa-Adebusoye). Patriarchal social factors enhance the position of males, thereby making it harder for females to compete on equal terms with their male colleagues. This was the submission of Fapohunda (1983), in his study of career ladder in Nigerian academia. Although the current study along that line by Olusi (1995) has not been concluded, available data suggest that the situation has not improved.

Section 3: Female-Immobility and Welfare: the Case of a University Labor Force.

The concept of mobility refers to the ease with which workers move from one occupation to another, or from a low position to a higher one, within the same occupation. While the first situation is referred to as horizontal mobility, or migration, the latter mobility is said to be vertical. Both of these have implications for welfare, since vertical promotions imply higher wages, and migration to other occupations, or geographic locations is often promoted within the same occupation as a very vital condition for welfare increase. The foregoing discussion had proved that female labors are not adequately represented in formal employment patterns, particularly in Third world countries like Nigeria. An examination of the mobility of labor force also shows that women's ability to move either vertically or horizontally is very much restricted in the less developed countries.

Employment in government establishments, are more often than not, based on educational qualifications, and there are no stated gender biases, regarding promotion of workers. In practice however, strong biases are implied. For instance, in a typical establishment, promotion will depend on the highest attained level of relevant education, experience—measured by the number of years worked for, some unstated goodwill of the university, academic promotion will depend on the number of published papers, in addition to these other ones. In a research conducted at Obafemi Awolowo University (Olusi, 1995), thirty academic members of staff were randomly selected. Only 7 of these are females. An examination of their promotion to their present position confirms that movement in the vertical direction is definitely slower for females. Starting as assistant lecturers in 1980, four of these female lecturers are still lecturer I, fifteen years after their first appointment, whereas, several of the male respondents reached the same position in 4 years!! All of the female respondents would want to remain in the university services, and have rarely gone on long leave of absence, while all male respondents have been away at some time or other, and would not mind working elsewhere for better pay. All female lecturers ascribe their slow movement to other commitments in their homes, particularly the care of children, which leaves little time for research and paper writing. Their wish to stay on, is based on their responsibility to their children's schooling, who they want to see conclude their studies before they (the mothers) consider other employments. A further investigation shows that by the time their last offspring leave school (primary to university), such mothers would have reached their ages of retirement, and it might be too late to move. Thus, such women have limited vertical mobility, and they are completely immobile horizontally. Perhaps a more relevant generalization from this study is the fact that these women's immobile conditions imply the near fixity of their incomes, even in the face of hard economic conditions, and hence a constraint on their household welfare. This same generalization can be made for most female workers in the formal sector. In Nigeria, there are thirty-one universities at present, but there is no female vice-chancellor, and there are very few female professors. The reasons often advanced for this are the same. However, discrimination which is also often given as a reason for women's immobility is more apparent in the private formal sector, than the government sector, where rules are not supposed to be gender biased, whereas they are, in practice.

From the foregoing it can be safely concluded that female labor is immobile. The pertinent question then is how do we effect changes in female mobility patterns? And this is discussed in the next section.

Section 4: Removing Female Labor Immobility: Some Salient Points.

The constraints imposed by various limitations to women's economic activities on development are in the process of being fully identified as earlier stated. Prominent among these limitations are unequal access to education, gender inequality in access to assets and services, land, extension services, and financial markets, among others. However constraints posed by female labor immobility have not been fully examined. This is because, it is always seen as a difficult problem to solve. The removal of all other constraints will help plunge women into the midstream of development, by making them take part in economic production. It is also to be noted however, that partaking in production is important, and it is the maximization of this participation that actually maximizes welfare, and development, which is the goal of all nations of the world. Thus, the removal of female labor immobility is also as necessary as the enhancement of female participation in production. It has been shown in this segment that educating women alone is not enough to ensure their household welfare, since they are not mobile. There are families in Nigeria where both parents are university graduates, but they cannot afford to feed their children properly, especially since the downturn of our economy. In most cases, opportunities exist for the woman to move out of her environment, or even look for a better employment abroad, but she is unable to, and hence the household continues to suffer. Female education may take households above the poverty line, it does not guarantee maximum welfare, since there are different rewards to labor in different parts of the world, and it is only through mobility of workers that the differences can be removed, and welfare maximized. Thus, it is necessary to remove those barriers to female labor mobility either in the vertical sense or in the horizontal sense, hence these suggestions:

Traditional Family Structure:

Women are charged with the responsibility of caring for their families, particularly cooking food and ensuring smooth schooling for their children. Government policies directed at attacking this set-up may meet with strong opposition from traditionalists. However, reforms of family law can enhance women's economic and social opportunities, while the cultural norms are still respected. For instance the minimum age of marriage can be set very high, so that apart from completing schooling, such girls will be able to work anywhere outside their homes before marriage. When children start to arrive, the provision of daycare centers and boarding schools could be made compulsory, so that mothers are able to go out to work anywhere. Female labor mobility will not be possible, and women may still need to spend time in cooking and home care technologies are not available. A woman who gets a better rewarding job, some distance away from home, should be able to prepare enough food to last for some days, and keep this in the deep freezer for the use of other members of her household. This will enhance her ability to earn more money, and at the same time still perform her normal duties in the home. Of course, this proposal may not be feasible in a country where there is incessant power failure, no pipe-borne water and where transportation system is not efficient. Hence for women to work at all, and to be mobile, policies should focus on providing relevant infrastructure.

Obviously, the most effective way of enhancing female mobility, and hence participation in development, is a change of the patriarchal sexual division of labor, such that men may become more involved in household chores. However, developing countries are not yet ready for such revolutionary changes, given the little effect of Western education on their traditional norms and beliefs. Men who help their wives at home are subjected to ridicule from friends and relatives. Hence it is common to see remarkable changes in men (who studied in advanced countries, and had helped their wives in household chores while there) as soon as they come back to their own countries.

Participation in Decision-Making:

Efforts to improve women's participation in development generally, and reduce their immobile status, so as to increase welfare, will of necessity involve seeking women's own view. This can be affected by actually making policies that ensure women's participation at the decision-making levels, at both the formal and informal sectors. A fair representation at such levels will remove some of the usual gender biases, and discrimination against women. Such often prevent their promotion and ability to seize opportunities to work outside, for better remuneration, which can improve their household's welfare. Highly educated women who have complained of lack of time to devote to their office or academic works, will obviously to release more time to such women to work for their promotion, on the one hand, and the provision of boarding schools for their children will enable them travel out of their homes, when necessary, for better rewarding jobs.

Women's Education:

Education is a very prominent variable for improving women's participation in development. However, as it has earlier been pointed out, women in most developing countries do not receive technical education. An improvement in the pattern of education will facilitate their mobility, since employments requiring such knowledge are not usually localized, and are highly rewarding in economic terms. The training of more women as engineers, pilots, computer engineers, and analysts, will definitely enhance income, and hence, welfare. Equally important is the encouragement of women in self-employment and entrepreneurship.

Social Relationship:

A major constraint on women's participation and mobility in particular is the view of women by men. In most societies, men see women as part of their possessions. This also has religious backings in most cases. Hence, the decision to work at all depends on the man. Unfortunately, most men see women's economic power as directly impinging on their authority. They do not recognize the welfare effects of their wives' income, and hence they oppose women's mobility in any form. This economic incapacitation no doubt represents a constraint on welfare increase in the home, the society and the country at large.

Perhaps, a solution to this is public enlightenment through the various news media, and more revolutionary actions on the part of women themselves.

CONCLUSION

This chapter has discussed the general work condition of women, particularly in developing countries, using Nigeria as proxy for others. Few women participate in the labor force, and suggestions have been made as to how the situation can be improved so that welfare increase can be secured.

CHAPTER TWENTY-FIVE

PRIVATIZATION AND COMMERCIALIZATION OF PUBLIC ENTERPRISES: THE RELEVANCE OF ADAM SMITH'S "INVISIBLE HAND IN DEVELOPING COUNTRIES."

PROFESSOR JANET OLUSI

INTRODUCTION

The main goal of all developing countries is to develop, since this enhances their standard of living. Hence countries seek the best strategies that can hasten the achievement of this goal. Usually, countries tend to employ strategies that were used in the present day developed countries in some years past, believing that they will work positively for them (the developing countries). It is for this reason that a revisit to the theories formulated by early economists, and which helped to accelerate the development of the developed countries becomes necessary.

Since the inception of classical economics over 200 years ago, one of the most sacred assumptions has been the hypothesis that an invisible hand determines market prices, which also follow a random walk. Economists of that time, led by Adam Smith, believed that division of labor would allow for increased specialization, and hence increased production to save mankind from its squalor and destitution (Olsen, 2001). Also Adam Smith believed that division of labor would only develop within the context of a free market economy, with competitive prices, not like the existing situation where government had firm control of market pricing.

Smith believed that to unleash the forces of the market and foster competition, it was necessary to free markets from government control. The ideas led him to propound the theory of invisible hand, which is discussed below.

The invisible hand.

The argument of the early economists in propounding the theory of perfect market, is that an efficient market has such a large volume, that any one participant has a negligible impact on the market as a whole. Since any single participant is so small, and insignificant, it was concluded that everyone behaved the same way. To the economists, man behaves like a "homo economic us" who is rational, and maximizes his utility. The implication of this is that everybody behaves the same way to market events, and that market reactions to outside events are homogeneous with no secondary reactions.

The invisible hand argument posits that overall allocation of resources by all markets is efficient, once they are perfectly competitive. This is because of the utility maximization ambition of all market participants, which is reflected, in the relative pricing of assets, and their allocation. What the invisible hand does, therefore, is that it links self-interest with public interest.

The implication of the above arguments is that once government hands off the market, invisible forces take over, to divert resources to their best alternative uses. It is assumed that the competitive atmosphere enhances economic development and the welfare of the citizenry. It is this argument that has informed the neo-liberal thinking, leading to the present day argument for globalization of the world's economy.

This chapter sets out to examine the correctness of this stance by early economists, and the relevance of their argument to the development drive of the developing countries, using Nigeria as a proxy for others. It examines the privatization and commercialization of public enterprises currently practiced, and seen as panacea for economic problems of poverty and inequality of income distribution in the country, as in most other developing countries. The rest of the chapter is divided into four (4) sections. Section 2 reviews the Nigerian economy, and highlights the conditions leading to the introduction of privatization and commercialization of public enterprises. Section 3 reviews the theoretical issues and existing literature on public and private sectors economic management dichotomy. Section 4 examines the status of privatization and commercialization policy implementation in Nigeria, and assesses the success of the scheme, and links this with the invisible hand. Section 5 concludes the chapter.

Section 2: Private and Public Enterprises in the Nigerian Economy.

The phenomenal increase in the price of Nigerian crude oil in the early 70's signified an unprecedented increase in the country's revenue earnings. This encouraged the policy makers in the country to invest some of the growing revenue to social, economic and physical investments, (Ayodele, 1994). It therefore signified a growing dominant role by the public sector in the Nigerian economy. By the 1980s the sector was already accounting for over 60% of modern sector employment, and 50% of the Gross Domestic Product. Public enterprises began to spring up in all areas of the economy, particularly sectors like mining, energy, transport, agriculture, manufacturing, commerce, social services and utilities. By 1985, there had developed about 70 non-commercial and over 100 commercial public enterprises at the Federal level alone (Ayodele, 1994). The other two tiers of government, state and local governments, also had their own shares of enterprises. Capital investments in such enterprises reached over N23 billion, made up of about N8billion in equity shares, and N15 billion in loans. Apart from this, the Federal government in Nigeria spent a high percentage of non-salary recurrent expenditure and capital investment budget on the maintenance and sustenance of the enterprises.

As a result of the collapse of crude oil prices in the late 1980's, which also led to the dwindling oil revenue in Nigeria, the country's fiscal and monetary posture became precarious, and uncertain. It became a luxury to maintain and sustain the country's large number of enterprises. The effects of this financial difficulty on the enterprise were inefficiencies, poor quality of services, and inappropriate financial returns. Most of the public enterprises performed below expectation, especially utilities like Water Corporation, Nigeria Railway Cooperation (NRC), Nigeria Airways, Nigerian International Telephone Exchange Limited (NITEL), Nigeria Postal Services (NIPOST) and the National Electric Power Authority (NEPA).

Financial returns on all these huge investments, were less than N 500 million annually. This was considered unfair by the Nigerian government. The requirement of the International Financial Organizations, and in particular International Monetary Fund (IMF 1985) and the World Bank (1983) and the structural adjustment drive, proposed total elimination of subsidies to these enterprises. It was also recommended that the public enterprises be categorized for subsequent reform, and full or partial privatization or commercialization. Nigeria accepted this suggestion for reform. In November 1987, the Council of States approved the recommendations made by the council of Ministers, to privatize or commercialize public enterprises. A number of reasons can therefore be advanced for the poor performance of public enterprises, and the subsequent withdrawal of government support for public enterprises through their privatization and commercialization. Such reasons include (a) insufficient autonomy, (b) inadequate or lack of performance measures, and appropriate incentives linked to performance (c) Bureaucratic rather than commercial-oriented management styles, (Commission Report 1984). The decision of government as well as the recommendations of the international financial organizations seem to have re-emphasized the economic stance of the invisible hand as the best assurance of welfare and it is in order to see how this can be best achieved that we need to search literature and theoretical assertions on the strategy of privatization and commercialization of public enterprises.

Section 3: Theoretical issues and literature on private and public sector management.

It has been said in the introduction that the classical economists assumed the efficacy of the invisible hand to allocate resources efficiently given the perfectly competitive thrust of the market. Privatization and commercialization have identical economic goals, which can be summarized as efficiency and profit maximization. However, the economic paradigm differs in concept. Privatization has been defined as a move by the public sector towards the pursuit of efficiency and effectiveness, in attainment of objectives, with a dominance of financial considerations through the adoption of management styles that reward good performance, and penalize poor performance, Kayode (1986) as quoted by Ayodele, (1994).

Commercialization, on the other hand equally aims at effectiveness, but through the move by the public sector, towards the adoption of the private enterprises style of management, Financial dominance (Kayode, 1986) as quoted by Ayodele, (1994).

Thus, in Nigeria, privatization of public concerns refers to the transfer of government equity shares in the ventures to private owners. Commercialization of public enterprises adopts government retainance of ownership of shares but ensures that the public pays for services rendered like in the private sector. Both can be said to aim at higher levels of performance, and one implies the other in the operational sense. However, it should be realized that commercialization may not imply privatization, when the structures of shares and ownership patterns are considered. Basically, there are both economic and political implications of the process involved in the management of both concepts. Economically, it is true that the main aim of both processes is resolvable to a single economic objective of profit maximization. In the area of politics however, the goals of equity embedded in the efficacy of the price system to allocate available resources becomes controversial. Thus the assumed perfection of the invisible hand in allocating resources to their best alternative uses becomes debatable, when used in an environment where politics dominates.

The conservatives, led by Friedman (1962), see government's participation in economic activities as inefficient, for the achievement of desired goals, and development of objectives. This is because of known inhibiting factors, like government's deficient bureaucratic organizational ability, and lack of efficiency and ineffectiveness in operational management. Summarily, the conservatives, like Adam Smith, recommend the reliance on market forces and by implication the invisible hand to make government move effective. The liberals express doubt in the ability of the invisible hand or the reliance on market forces to allocate available resources efficiently. Galbraith (1978) highlights the limitations of the price system, which government intervention can suppress through regulatory bodies. Sometimes, subsidization policies, and the provision of social services, and utilities, are best made by government, since the private sector is averse to the provision of such. The private sector always engages in cut-throat sales promotion, and advertising, which make consumers buy goods, which they rarely need. Hence, the price system engages in the use of coercion to allocate goods and services, in a way that only those who can afford the equilibrium prices buy. This implies that the poor who constitute the larger half of the societies in the LDCs are not able to buy even the basic needs of life. This is because income distribution in such countries is skewed against majority of citizens. This condition is regarded by Samuelson (1983), as a form of coercion, and the situation, according to the liberals, is regarded as sociopolitical injustice, (Ayodele 1994).

In a way, the Nigerian situation reflects the use of a mixture of these two conflicting arguments. The establishment of public enterprises in the 1970's with heavy subsidization polices is tantamount to accepting the arguments of the liberals. On the other hand, events leading to the adoption of Structural Adjustment Policy (SAP) prove the liberals wrong. This is because the public enterprises performed poorly, and these as reflected in low and declining productivity, capacity underutilization of plants along with the socio-economic crisis of the 1980s and the poor financial situation imposed harsh economic situation on Nigerians. SAP rationalizes the argument of the conservatives on the reliance on market forces, and hence the invisible hand for resources allocation.

Section 3b: Theoretical argument for the existence of problems of public enterprises in Nigeria.

The aforementioned undesirable characteristics of public enterprises arose from the policies enacted to regulate their activities and a budgetary resource flows between the public enterprises and government. While government fulfilled its financial obligations, the PES did not honor their suggesting flows in the policies (lwayemi, 1992, Ayodele 1987 and 1982).

Regulatory policies include subsidization, debt guarantee, foreign/local borrowing, tax and subvention policies. There is no doubt that the policies have contributed to the observed inefficiencies in public enterprises, operational or technical. Such inefficiencies include production, allocation, financial, pricing and institutional based, on the modern economic theories regarding the relationship between economic behavior and public ownership of institutions, (Eggertson 1990).

According to the X-efficiency hypothesis of Libeinstein, (1966), the manager of a business enterprise would attain the highest level of efficiency when his autonomy is assured. Also the property rights theory highlights the relationship between government as well as owners of PEs on the one hand and the managers and workers of the enterprise on the other hand. If the relationship between the two groups does not give the desired business management authority to the PEs managers, difficulties would be created in achieving the interests of both. X-inefficiency hypothesis highlights the degree of inefficiencies linked with the public ness of PEs while the agency theory discusses the need to grant unreserved autonomy to PEs managers in order to reduce the degree of X-inefficiency problems associated with them. Lack of shared information between governments and PEs managers impedes governments from monitoring their performance or providing appropriate incentives to them. Consequently, the managers have less drive and efficiency, hence, they only try to meet the minimum standards set by government which is usually a far cry from their actual potentials.

The X-inefficient position posits that an enterprise cannot produce a given level of output at the lowest cost possible under the existing state of production technology and input supply condition.

The results are losses of welfare to the community. This then explains the problems of public enterprise in a country like Nigeria, particularly before the Structural Adjustment Program (SAP) period. During the pre SAP period governments of the country intervened frequently in the operation of PEs particularly in matters relating to pricing investment, technological choices and projects selections. Besides delays in executing projects were experienced given the bureaucratic form of executing policies. The lack of independence by PEs managers explains therefore why the PEs operated inefficiently thus paving way for the ensuing institutional reforms via commercialization and privatization policy (Galal 1991)

Section 4.: An assessment of the effects of Commercialization and Privatization of Public Enterprise on the Nigerian Economy.

Having discussed the antecedents of privatization and commercialization policy in Nigeria, it is necessary to see how the policy has faired since its inception in 1986. As a first step, the modality for privatization and commercialization need to be examined. In the first place it should be noted that SAP proposed to adjust enterprises' multidimensional and resolve conflicting objectives by imposing the singular objective of profit maximization in the private enterprise.

Secondly, it was intended to make the enterprises free from ministerial controls. Thus they will be financially independent and effective in the administration sense. This is why it is believed that privatization and commercialization leads to increase in user charges of utilities produced by them. One major socio-economic justification for the commercialization and privatization policy is that the attendant improved efficiency brings about expansion in output, which may meet the rising demand for public goods. One underlying assumption is that the private sector is a more efficient producer than the public sector.

Decree No 25 of October 1986 on commercialization and privatization of public enterprises gave legal framework to the policy. The main objective of commercialization and privatization include: the establishment of a Technical Committee on Commercialization and privatization (TCPC) to oversee the management of the program. Thereafter, TCPC categorized the enterprise into those for full commercialization, partial commercialization, full privatization, and partial privatization.

(a) Fully commercialized enterprises operate as full commercial enterprises, which set their prices appropriately to operate at profit.
(b) Partially commercialized ones are expected to cover their operating costs.
(c) Fully privatized enterprises feature full divestiture of all federal government equity interests.
(d) Partial privatization signifies the sale of a proportion of government equity to the public.
(e) Public establishments where the ownership of affected enterprises remained with the federal government, which provides the necessary investible funds. The above categories represent the signal for advancing the concept and involving the citizens in operation of the enterprise hitherto belonging to the federal government in Nigeria. The extent of involvement determines the welfare of the citizens.

(a) <u>Effects on Welfare.</u>

The Structural Adjustment Policies of privatization and commercialization of PEs aimed at insulating the enterprises from governments' bureaucratic and shifting control, and impose the objective of profit maximization within the mixed economic system of Nigeria. This creates the impression that the commercialization and privatization is synonymous with increases in user charges for social service, and utilities produced, (Ayodele 1994). This has had serious implication on the welfare of the citizens, as demonstrated in figures 1 and 2.

In figure 1, increases in user charges reduce the magnitude of consumers' surplus AP_1B_1 to AP_2C. Hence; a loss of $P_2CB_1P_1$ is recorded. Goods purchased declined from Oq_2 to $Oq1$. The loss of q_1q_2 is recorded due to the reduction of consumers' income. OP_1 was the subsidized price while OP_2 represents the privatized commercialized price (subsidies have been eliminated).

In figure 2, the consumers' budget line rolled backwards changing their equilibrium quantities from E (high utility level) to B (low utility level) thus signifying a loss of welfare.

One of the best enterprises to demonstrate this loss in welfare is the Nigeria Airways, which increased fare in October 1987. The immediate effect was its operating less than full capacity, the company no longer broke-even financially, and it is now grounded as a result of this, workers were retrenched, while the high level manpower, that is pilots and engineers, had to resign their appointments. This is equally true of most other enterprises and the result is the rescheduling of their operations to the only profitable ventures, which do not often benefit the masses and hence do not promote the rate of development. For instance, rural water supply and rural electrification schemes were popular in the mid 90's in Nigeria, but these became threatened with privatization and commercialization. Since rural citizens could not pay, the cost of such utilities when government subsidies became drastically reduced or removed, and hence the projects could not continue. The reduced welfare effects of lack of water and electricity cannot be overemphasized, in terms of reducing rates of development and imparting undesirable economic conditions on Nigerians.

The primary goal of the privatization and commercialization program is to make the private sector the leading engine of growth of the Nigerian economy. The government intends to use the privatization program to reintegrate Nigeria back into the global economy, as a platform to attract foreign direct investment in an open, fair and transparent manner. The specific objectives of the privatization and commercialization programs are:

(1) To send a clear message to the local and international community that a new transparent Nigeria is now open for business.

(2) To restructure and rationalize the public sector in order to substantially reduce the dominance of unproductive government investment in the sector.

(3) To change the orientation of all public enterprises engaged in economic activities towards a new horizon of performance, improvement, viability and overall efficiency.

(4) To raise funds for financing socially-oriented programs, such as poverty eradication, health, education and provision of infrastructure.

(5) To ensure positive returns on public sector investment in commercialized enterprises, through more efficient private sector-oriented management.

(6) To check the present absolute dependence on the treasury for funding by otherwise commercially oriented parastatals, and so, encourage their approach to the Nigerian and international capital markets to meet their funding needs.

(7) To initiate the process of gradual cession to the private sector of public enterprises, which are better operated by the private sector.

(8) To create jobs, acquire new knowledge, skills and technology, and expose Nigeria to international competition.

An objective assessment of the effects of commercialization and privatization can only be made after considering their performance alongside the objectives they set out to achieve.

EFFECTS ON OWNERSHIP PATTERN/ DISTRIBUTIONAL EFFECTS

The Technical Committee on Privatization and Commercialization (TCPC), has since metamorphosed into the Bureau of public enterprises (BPE). It should be noted that policy of commercialization and privatization passed through stages. This pace is dictated by the government of the day who may or may not be fully disposed to the market-oriented reform. Thus the program implementation has been epileptic in Nigeria and since 1999, Government's interest has again been rekindled in the program. Of course this was partly due to the preconditions set by the International Monetary Fund (IMF) for negotiating an interim program monitored by fund staff that would open the way for talks on a medium term economic strategy agreement for Nigeria. Nigeria also needed an accord with IMF and the World Bank to pave the way for debt relief tasks with the Paris club, whose membership alone, account for 70 percent of the country's total foreign debt of about \$31 bn (in 1996).

A quick breakdown of the first group of enterprises scheduled for privatization gives the information in the following tables. The first table consists of enterprises in which equity held were to be partially privatized. Under the program government planned to sell 40 percent of its equity to "Strategic investors" usually foreigners who would also manage the concerns.

Another 20 percent were to go to Nigerian investors while government retained 40 percent of equity shares.

Table 1

Enterprise sector	No of enterprises	Maximum strategic participation percent	Federal govt. participation percent of total	Nigeria individuals participation percent of total
Telecommuni-cation	2	40	40	20
Electricity	1	40	40	20
Petroleum	6	40	40	20
Fertilizer	2	40	40	20
Machine tools	1	40	40	20
Gas	1	40	40	20
Steel Aluminium	6	40	40	20
Mining solid materials	4	40	40	20
Media	2	40	40	20
Insurance	2	40	40	20
Papers	3	40	40	20
Sugar	3	40	40	20
Total	33			

In all 33 companies were to be partially privatized in the first scheduled 48 public enterprises consisting of hotels, cement companies, commercial and merchant banks, motor oil vehicle assembly plants etc were to be fully privatized.

In the second schedule, 24 public enterprises were to be partly commercialized.

As indicated in the table, the biggest companies to go on auction block were the National Electric Power Authority and Nigeria Telecommunications (NITEL), which are Nigeria's second and third largest public corporations, after the giant Nigerian National Petroleum Corporation (NNPC). Others include National Fertilizer Company, hotels, steel rolling mills, and oil refineries, which were also to be privatized. It is against the background of the foregoing information that effects of privatization are measured. Three important areas are considered. The first is the effect of P&C on welfare. This has been discussed earlier.

Secondly, effects of P&C on equity.

Equity: The issue of balancing equity holdings in P&C are two fold. (1) Nigeria is a heterogeneous country, with many ethnic groups, and this is often reflected in her sharing of national resources. (2) The achievement of equity in income distribution as a developmental goal requires the assurance that companies' equity shares be transferred to the poor, to enhance their income, and that the pricing policy of commercialized enterprises be fair to them. This is important in a country where income distribution is skewed against the poor.

The achievement of equity has delayed to a large extent, the privatization of some states enterprises. There is ample evidence that even the privatized companies had gone into the hands of the rich. Equity shares were offered through the stock exchange, where low-income earners are scarcely ever found. Although strategies like nationwide distributions of application forms to post offices, local government head quarters, state offices and state ministries of commerce and industries were said to have been employed, in addition, limits were placed on the number of shares that could be purchased by individuals. It is pertinent here to say that widespread poverty would have frustrated the aims of achieving a good spread of ownership or equity. It is note worthy however that by 1992, 32 of these enterprises were sold, through public offers. Various methods were used to ensure equitable distribution of the shares and to encourage small investors. It has been reported that well over half a million new shareholders were created in Nigeria, thereby strengthening the capital market, but this questions the shares sold, included those of 12 privatized banks and every local government in the country has shareholders. In fact there is said to be a shareholders Association organized into seven zones in the country (Africa recovery 1998). The fears of job losses or concentration of wealth in a few hands, were said to have not been confirmed.

However, it should be noted that the foregoing deals with small enterprises. The total of returns on the sale of such enterprises is less that government's holdings in any one big enterprises like National Electric Power Authority (NEPA)

The status of such has been frustrated by the social economic condition of Nigeria. This includes widespread corruption, inefficiency, poor infrastructure and generally difficult business environment, which discourages foreign investors who could buy them. Hence NEPA, Nigeria Airways, NITEL etc are awaiting privatization even though same degree of commercialization has been done for some of them.

(b) Effects on the performance of enterprises

Product prices of affected enterprises have all risen astronomically. Obadan (1998). This is confirmed on table 2.

Table 2: Tariff Trends in selected privatizes enterprises in Nigeria (1985–1995)

PEs	Product	Unit of Measures	1985	1989	1990	1991	1992	1995	1995 Index (1985 = 100)
NEPA	Electricity	Kwh	0.06	0.11	0.29	0.32	0.32	0.53	883
NNPC	L.P.G	13Kg	5.00	80.00	80.00	80.00	120.00	250.00	5,000
	P.M.S	Litere	0.20	0.40	0.60	0.70	0.70	11.00	5,000
	Kerosene	Litere	0.15	0.15	0.40	0.50	0.50	9.00	6,000
	Fuel Oil	Litere	0.30	30.00	30.00	35.00	35.00	85.00	28,333
NIPOST	Postal Service	Postage s	0.20	0.50	0.50	0.50	0.50	5.00	2,500
	Registry tion		0.50	1.50	1.50	1.50	1.50	30.00	6,000
NITEL	Som. Rwlw & Telex	Pulses	0.10	0.10	0.90	0.90	0.90	5.00	5,000
	Inter. Telex & Telex	Minutes	3.00	3.00	23.00	23.00	23.00	40.00	1,333

Source: Central Bank of Nigeria: *Annual Reports and Statement of Accounts,* 1985–1995

The table shows that product prices have risen. The least price increase within the period of analysis is electricity whose index was about 88.3 in 1995. While others have theirs above 5000 (e.g. LPG/PMS, kerosene and NITEL services). Their trends have arisen from the cost consciousness of enterprises hence there have been a check on resources wastage the PEs are more sensitive under c and p. it can therefore be said and c&p have made the enterprises more competitive and their earnings have increased.

The invisible hand and Nigeria commercialization and privatization policy.

In spite of the salutary effects of C & P presented above, there is a strong doubt if the purported advantages expected from the policy are fully realized and hence a strong doubt on the advantages of the invisible hand. By 1996, about $2.4bn or 100 billion Naira had been invested by the federal government in public enterprises with an average rate of returns of only about 2 per cent. (Africa Recovery, 1998).

The recorded disappointments derive from factors related to the implementation problems and several socio-economic and political constraints. Some of these are discussed below:

(i)   Inefficiency of commercialized PEs: The withdrawal of subsidies was to make the enterprises economically efficient. Events have proved that even though tariffs increased by 1000 percent in some PEs yet the imbalances in the PEs markets remain intractable. Enterprises like NEPA, NITEL, NRC (Nigerian Railway Corporation) and NIPOST still render unimpressive services to the nation hence the invisible hand can be said to have failed in achieving efficiency.

(ii) Irregular maintenance of equipment: It was expected that the management of commercialized

(iii) PEs would adopt better methods of maintaining their equipment so as to improve performance. This has not been so judged by the incessant power failure of NEPA and fuel shortages of the NNPC all of which have been partly attributed to poor maintenance of equipment.

(iv) The absence of an effective supervisory system.: The bureau of public enterprises supervises the entire program but there are no parallel bodies to supervise the enterprises hence their non-compliance with the performance agreement is not checked. This results in all other vices seen in the operations of the public enterprises after commercialization.

(v) Political Interference: Commercialization program is seriously affected by the influence of political interests. Management and Boards of PEs are changed while the supervising ministries do not adhere to the roles provided for them in the agreement. The result is that the PEs are still run as before and this frustrates performance.

(vi) Inability to raise funds from the local capital market without government approval: The reform had envisaged that commercialized enterprises should be able to raise funds through local and external capital markets without government guarantee but this has not been so. This is because such enterprises have not been granted the required autonomy, there is lack of commitment on the part of executors and government lost interest in the program for sometime between 1993 and 1996. The result of all these limitations is the inability of the enterprises to perform as expected after reform.

Privatization and the Invisible hand

As a result of some operational limitations, "the invisible hand" has not been seen working in the privatized enterprises for the following reasons;

a) Shareholding in the PEs were expected to follow some geo-political distri-
    bution pattern, this has not been so. Some ethnic groups have consistently
    dominated the ownership of equity shares in the PEs. Achievement of
    equity in the distribution of income is therefore frustrated in the process.
b) Most interested buyers of PEs equity shares cannot do so because of lack of
    credit. Although, banks were directed to give loans for such purposes, they
    remain disobedient to the Central Banks' authority. Consequently, only the
    rich can buy PEs equity shares thus creating wider gaps between the rich
    and the poor
c) Large Institutional investors rather than small individual investors sub-
    scribe to the offer of shares. In a country where over 70% live below the
    poverty line, the inequitable effects cannot be over emphasized.
d) Foreign investors have not been attracted in large number probably due
    to lack of conducive atmosphere in terms of infrastructure and needed
    confidence in the Nigerian economy which is ruled by political and social
    upheavals. Some policy issues have also emerged as limitations in the work-
    ings of the invisible hand. Such includes non-incorporation of commer-
    cialized enterprises giving them opportunities to retain their monopoly
    powers. Monopolies have never promoted development. The rule of thumb
    rather than the forces of supply and demand is engaged in charging tariffs
    arbitrarily. Moreover, the enterprises are not fully autonomous and had
    no boards in most cases. It is obvious from the foregoing that the expected
    performance of the invisible hand has been truncated by all these limita-
    tions in Nigeria thus making a mockery of the proclaimed salutary effects
    of the "hand" as propounded by the classical economics. Perhaps, this is
    the reason why the new neo-liberal agenda of globalization is also being
    frustrated in Africa in general since privatization and trade liberalization
    are central to the efficient and effective performance of the phenomenon.

Recommendations

Recommendations for improvement of this all-important program is expedi-
ent, because of its importance in launching Nigeria into its rightful place in
the world's economy. Main areas of improvement concern the capital market,
ownership base, government roles and timing of the program. These are discussed briefly below.

The Nigeria capital Market: One of the foremost needs is to adequately equip
the capital market for the absorption of equity shares that emerge from C and

P of public enterprises. Right now, the market does not seem to be equipped in terms of manpower, adequate techniques, finance and experience. There is need to recruit new hands and old staff who do not have knowledge of modern methods of transaction in the market.

Ownership base: So far the methods used in the sale of equity shares of PEs have ensured the dominance of the rich and institutional bodies in the owner-ship patterns. Preference should be given to small-scale investors distributed in order to alleviate poverty all over the country. Labor Unions, cooperative societies and grass root unions in general should be given access to govern-ment shares that are sold in the PEs. If possible, wards in local governments and traditional rulers should be involved to ensure fair distribution of the shares. Some associations are now offering loans to citizens to help them pur-chase shares in the privatized companies. To this effect, a scheme referred to as the Privatization Share Purchase Loan scheme has been designed to enable Nigerians particularly the low-income bracket have the opportunity to par-ticipate in the privatization program of the National council; on privatization (NCP). The effect of this scheme is yet to be seen as it was inaugurated in the year 2003, which is still too recent for an objective assessment to be made on its impact. However, it is strongly believed that if well implemented, the Loan Scheme will aid the achievement of the objectives of equity and poverty allevia-tion in Nigeria.

Setting up of a team of experts: There is a need to set up a team of experts, to ensure the achievement of the desired objectives of C and P, which are job creation, acquisition of new knowledge, skills and technology, and exposing the country to international competition. In other words, the team should ensure the working of the invisible hand in directing and controlling the resources and directing production patterns in the economy.

Setting up of a Nigerian Trust Fund: There is no doubt that proceeds from privatization have been very huge and will still continue to increase. Mismanagement of such funds should be prevented by setting up a trust fund that will ensure that the funds are invested within and outside the country. Such investment will provide employment, as well as expand the economy base for Nigeria. Also such funds can improve education, health, agriculture and other sectors of the economy. Moreover, the share ownership of Nigerians in the privatized enterprise can be financed using such funds.

In other words, the "invisible hand" may not function properly, if not aided by some visible hands, to start with.

CONCLUSION.

This concluding chapter has revisited the classical assumption of the efficacy of the "invisible hand" manifesting through economic reforms of privatization and commercialization of public enterprises. It is upheld by classical economists, led by Adam smith, that the withdrawal of government from economic activities, and the dominance of the forces of supply and demand lead, to quicker achievement of development. Theories in support of this stance have been revisited, while the Nigerian commercialization and privatization of public enterprises have been used as a test case for the philosophy of the invisible hand. The extensive review of the program, and the analysis have proved that even though it is capable of achieving the set goals of poverty reduction, equitable distribution of income, full employment etc. as Adam Smith predicted, Nigeria is yet to realize these goals, and hence, it remains a fallacy in the country. Institutional problems have risen to frustrate the workings of the program, hence, the macro problems of inflation, unemployment, and inequitable income distribution still persist in the country.

Political upheavals on the workings of P & C are very common. The chairmanship of the bureau has caused a lot of wrangling in recent times. Efforts wasted in these debates and political struggles, can be better spent on planning better strategies for privatization and commercialization of enterprises, to achieve its statutory objectives, particularly that of allowing the invisible hand to link the interests of all participants in the economy, with the achievement of growth and development.

Conclusively, it is sure that the invisible hand recommended by the early economists is taking hold in most developing countries. Judging by the case of Nigeria, the phenomenon is quite relevant, but the good effects have not been fully achieved, because of some institutional limitations, such as political, technological, financial and management problems. This makes it necessary for the "hand" to be supported by the invisible hand of government policies at the initial stage, while its independent relevance can only be achieved gradually, if the existing problems of poverty, inequality, and low rate of development are to be solved.

SUGGESTED READINGS

Adamson, R.G. (1971): <u>Pollution An Ecological Approach.</u> Bellhaven Hose Limited.

Adeyanju, L.J. (1995) Importance of Teacher Education, Today and the Future. <u>Journal of Nigerian Association for Educational Media and Technology.</u> (JEMT) Vol.5 No 1 pp 27, 34.

Adetula, L.O. (1990): Language Factor: Does it affect Children's Performance on Word Problems? <u>Educational Studies in Mathematics</u> 21:351-365.

Adekanye, Tomilayo (1993): "<u>Population, Environment and Development: The Policy Option</u>"; Paper presented at the National Seminar on Population and the Environment; Organized by the Foundation for Environmental Development and Education in Nigeria (FEDEN); 5th May, 1993.

Adekanye T.O.; Awoyemi, T.T.; Okoruwa V. (1995): <u>The Socio-Economic Status of African Women in Agriculture.</u> Paper Presented at the Fourth General Assembly and Seminar of the Association of Africa Women for Research and Development (AAWORD) in Pretin, South Africa 7th–11th April.

Adetoro J.E. (1985): <u>Historical Development of Vocational and Technical Education in Nigeria.</u> N.E.R.A Lagos.

Aina, O.I. (1995): "Nigerian Women in the Urban Labor Force: Trends and Issues" In <u>Nigerian Women in Social Change</u>, edited by Simi Afonja and Bisi Aina, Obafemi Awolowo University Press, Ile-Ife, Nigeria.

Akujuru, V.A. (1999): The Professional Duty of the Valuer in Oil Pollution Compensation Valuation. <u>Journal of Nigerian Affairs.</u>

Alfred G. (1992): <u>Sexually Transmitted Diseases</u>. Lagos.

Appel, W. (1983): <u>Cults in America</u>. New York & Winston.

Anyanwu, J.C. (2005) Rural Poverty in Nigeria: Profile, Determinants and Exit Paths. African Development Review

Awe, Bolanle (1993): "Gender, Culture, Poverty and Environment" Paper Presented at the National Seminar on Poverty and the Nigerian Environment. Organized by the Foundation for Environmental Development and Education in Nigeria (FEDEN) and the Rockefeller Foundation Lagos.

Ayodele, A. (1987): Public Enterprises and the Structural Adjustment Program: Policy Implementation and Implication, in Structural Adjustment Program in a Developing Country, Economy. The Case of Nigeria. Eds Adedokun O.; Philips, I; and Ndekwu E. Nigerian Institute of Social and Economic Research Ibadan.

Ayorinde, Akolawole (1963): Mental Health and Everyday Living: An Insight into Practical Issues of Life, Lagos. Nigeria.

Azikwe N.B. (1934): How shall we educate the African? Journal of the African Society. Lagos No 3. P. 147.

Bardasi, E.: Wordon, D. (2006) Measuring Time Poverty and Analyzing its Determinants, Concepts and Application to Guinea, in Gender, Time Use and Poverty in Sub Saharan Africa. World Bank Working Paper. No 73.

Baruhart, C. L.; Barhhart, R.K.; The World Book Dictionary.

Beck, H.F. (1995): The Cults. St Louis: CPH

Bernstein, J. et al (2005) Brief Motivational Intervention at a Clinic visit reduces Cocaine and Heroine use. Drugs and Alcohol Dependence. 77. (1): 49-59

Bisong, J.O. (1999): New Syllabus Effective English for Junior Secondary Schools. Book 1. Evans Brothers Nig. Publishers Ibadan

Blackden, C.M.: Wodon, O. (2006) Gender Time Use and Poverty in Sub Saharan Africa. World Bank Working Paper.

Borisade, A.B. (2002): The New Partnership for Africa's Development (NEPAD) in ADEA Newsletter. 14 (4) 12-14

Boserup, E. (1970): Women's role in Economic Development; St. Martins Press New York.

Boru, L. Tomori, S.H.O. (1979): Handbook of Adult Education in West Africa. London: Hutchinson University Library for Africa.

Brauner, C.J., Burns, H.W. (1965): Problems in Education and Philosophy. New York.

Bouis, H., Haddard L. (1990): Effects of Agricultural Commercialization in Land Tenure Household (IFPRI) 79 Resource Allocation and Nutrition in the Philippines.

Brodemeir, H.C.; Stephenson, R.M. (1969): The Analysis of Social Systems.

Brim, O.G.; Wheeler, S. (1966): Socialization After Childhood. Wiley, Good Survey and Analysis of Adult Socialization.

Bush R.L. (1954) The Teacher Pupil Relationship. Englewood Cliffs, N.J. Prentice Hall, Inc.

Cassen, R.H. (2004) Development Economics. The Microsoft Corporation. Microsoft Encarta. 2003

Coleman, J.S. (1963): Nigeria's Background to Nationalism. University of California Press.

Commission Report (1984): Report of the Commission on Federal Government of Nigeria Statutory Corporation and state-owned corporation. Lagos. Nigeria.

Convey, R.A.; Ross, R.D. (1980): Handbook of Industrial Waste Disposal. Van Nostrand Reinhold Co.

Christine, O. (1993): Labor and Population. Working Papers of the World Employment Program ILO. Geneva.

Cressey, D.R. (1975): The Prison: Studies in Institutional Organization and change.

Curtis, S.V.; Boultwood, M.E.A. (1953): A Short History of Educational Ideas. University Tutorial Press.

Drug Enforcement Administration (2006) Get it Straight: The Facts about Drugs.

Due, F.M. (1986): Agricultural Policy in Tropical Africa: Is a Turn-around Possible? Illinois. Agricultural Economics Staff Paper 86. E. Urbana, Champaign. University of Illinois.

Eyibe, S.C. (1995): The Burden and Menace of Secret Cults in Higher Education. National Light. Sunday July, 30.

Ezeah, P.C. (2001): The Menace of Secret Cults in Higher Educational Institutions in Nigeria: Causes, Consequences and solutions. Crises and Challenges in Higher Education in Developing Countries, A Book of Readings. (eds.) Akubue, A.U.; Eny; D. Nsukka.

Evans, Mary (1994): The Women Question. Sage Publication.

Fedeiye, Dele (1978): Current Affairs and Essays in social Studies Olufemi Pres.

Fapohunda E.R. (1983): "Female and Male Work Profiles" in Oppong (ed) Female and Male in West Africa; London: George Allen and Unwin.

Fafunwa, A. Babs (1974): History of Education in Nigeria. George Allen and Unwin.

Fafunwa, A. B.; Macauley, J.K.; Sokoya, J.A. (1989): Education in mother Tongue: The Ife Primary Education Research Project (1970–1976) Ibadan University Press.

Farrank, J.S. (1964): Principles and Practice of Education. Longman.

Federal Republic of Nigeria Social Statistic (1985): Federal Office of Statistics.

Fofack, H. (2002) The Nature and Dynamics of Poverty. World Bank Working Paper. No 2847. Washington D.C.

Foote, Nelson; Cottrell, L.S. (1955): Identity and Interpersonal Competence. University Chicago Press.

Friedman, M. (1962): Capitalist and Freedom. University of Chicago Press.

Federal Republic of Nigeria (1992) Environmental Impact Assessment Decree No 86, Gazette No 73, vol 79. Federal Government Printer, Lagos.

Federal Republic of Nigeria (1998): National Policy on Education Lagos. Federal Environmental Impact

Federal Environmental Protection Agency (FEPA) (1995): Environmental Impact Assessment Procedural Guidelines Abuja.

Galbraith J.K. (1978) Affluent Society. New American Library. New York.

Gladwin, H.G. (1991) ed. Structural Adjustment and African Women Farmers; (ed) Christian H. Gladwin. University of Florida Press, Center for African Studies.

Good, Carter (1959): Dictionary of Education. McGraw Hill.

Gesell, A. (1940): The First Five Years. Harper and Row.

Haralambos, M. Heald, R.M. (1980): Sociology: Themes and Perspectives.

Havighurst, R.J. (1981) The Teaching Profession. Encyclopedia Britannica. Pp 9-16.

Hilgard, E.R. (1977) Theories of Learning. Englewood Cliffs, N.J. Prentice Hall

Hirst, P.H.; Peters, R.S. (1970): The Logic of Education. Routledge and Kegan Paul. London.

Ifeoma, E. (2001): Curbing Secret Cults Dimension Crisis in Nigerian Universities, in Crises and Challenges in Higher Education in Developing countries, A Book of Readings. (eds) Akubue, O.; Enyi 1. Nsukka.

Ijere, M.O. (1991): Women in Nigerian Economy, Accra publishers, Lagos.

Ikhariale, M.A. (1998): A Constitutional Imperative on the Environment: A Program of Action for Nigeria. Lagos.

Isichie, A.O., Suford, W.W. (1976): The Effects of Waste Gas Flares on the Surrounding Vegetation ion the South Eastern Nigeria. Journal of Applied Ecology. 13. pp. 177-187.

Kennedy, E. (1989): The Effects of Sugarcane Production on Food Security, Health and Nutrition in Kenya, A Conjectural Analysis (IFPRI).

Kirkpatrick, E.M. (1983): Chambers 20th Century Dictionary. Spectrum Books.

Knowles, M. (1973): The Adult Learner: A Neglected Species. Gulf Publishing Company. Houston.

Knox, A.B. (1981): Adult Development and Learning. Jossey—Bass Publisher. San Francisco.

Laftorich, R.H. (1973): The Price Systems and Resource Allocation. The Dryden press. London.

Levin, S.V. (1980): Youth and Religious Cults: A Social and Clinical Dilemma in Adolescent Psychiatry (eds).

Liberstein (1966) Allocation Efficiency Versus X-Efficiency. American Economic Review. Vol 56, pp 392-415.

Mayo, (2005) Drug Addiction. Mayo Foundation for Medical education and
Research

Mkandawire, T. (1989): Structural Adjustment And Agrarian Crisis in Afica: A
Research Agenda. Working Paper 2.

Miller, M.R., Rose, H.C.; (1975): Instructors and their Jobs. American Technical
Society Chicago III. U.S.A.

Morgan, C.T.: King R.L. (1975) Introduction to Psychology. Rinehart and
Kegan Paul. New York.

Nancy, F. (1995): Holding Hands at Midnight The Paradox of Caring Labor in
Feminist Economics. Vol 1 No. 1 Spring Bell and Bain Glasgow.

Newsman, P.A. (2004) Education and economic Development. Microsoft
Encarta Premium. Microsoft Corporation.

Nigerian Ten-Year Development Plan (1986) The Government Printer Lagos.

Ndoye, M. (2002): Development Cooperation, New Initiatives, New Trends in
(ADEA).

Nwazuoke, I.A. (2004) Challenging Adolescent Exuberance to Creative Exploits.
In Contemporary Issues and Researches on Adolescents. Ed Nwazuoke, I.A.;
Bamgbose, Y. & Moronkola, O.A. Royal People Nig. Ltd. Ibadan. Nigeria

Obadari, M. Ayodele, A. (1998): Commercialization and Privatization Policy in
Nigeria. National Center for Economic Management and Administration
(NCEMA). Ibadan.

Okojie, C. (2003) Gender and Education as Determinants of Household Poverty
in Nigeria, in Perspective on Growth and Poverty. Tokyo and New York. U N
University Press pp 268–295

Novicki, M.A. (2004): Boosting Basic Education in Africa. In Africa Recovery
Online.

Obanewa, O; (1999): "Adult Literacy Campaign in A rural Setting", in
Contemporary Issues in Educational Theory and Practice in Nigeria, edited
by C.N. Anyawu and O. Obanewa Ibadan: AMFITOP Books, pp. 1-9.

Ofodile, C. (2001); "Crises and Challenges in Higher Education in Developing
countries Students' Factor: Cultism", in Crises and Challenges in Higher
Education in Developing countries, A Book of Readings, edited by

A.U. Akubue and D. Enyi, Nsukka: A Publication of the Department of Educational foundations, University of Nigeria. Pp. 309-317.

Okirika, V.N. (2001): "Ethical Challenges of Cultism in Nigerian Education: Examination of an Aspect of the Crises and Challenges in Higher Education", in Crises and Challenges in Higher Education in Developing countries, A Book of Readings, edited by A.U. Akubue and D. Enyi, Nsukka: A Publication of the Department of Educational foundations, University of Nigeria. Pp. 326-334.

Okorodudu, I.R. (1999): "Attitude Development and Its Implications for Adult Counseling and Education in Nigeria" in Contemporary Issues in Educational Theory and Practice in Nigeria, edited by C.N. Anyanwu and O. Obanewa Ibadan: AMFITOP pp. 281-296.

Olukoya, S. (1997): "Terrorism on Campuses", Newswatch, February 24, 1997, pp. 7-11.

Olusi Janet (1995): "Gender Inequity and Inequality of Income Distribution: Any hope for improvement in 3rd World Countries?; Paper presented at the 4th Annual Conference for Feminist Economics, Tours, France, 5–7 July.

Olusi Janet (1995): "The Vital Recourse between Women's Poverty and Access to State Apparatus in Independent Africa"; Evidence from Nigeria. Paper Presented at the 4th General Assembly of Association of African Women for research and Development held in Pretoria, South Africa 7–11th April, 1995.

Olsen, Richart (2001): High Frequency Finance. Academic Press.

Opubor, A.E. (2000): Communication Development and Education Some Linkages. In Association in Africa. (ADEA) Newsletter 4 (10) 2, 1-4.

Orhen, A. (1994): Learning mathematical Issues. Theories and Classroom Practice. New York Cassell.

Orton, A.; Wan, G. (1994): Issues in Teaching Mathematics. New York. Cassell.

Otterburn, M.K.; Nicholson, A.R. (1976): The Language of (CSE) Mathematics. Mathematics in Schools 5(5) 18-20

Onycmunwa, S.G. (1998): "The Emerging Roles and Qualities of Adult Educators", in Handbook of Education for Nigeria, edited by C.N. Anyanwu, Ibadan: AMFITOP pp. 91-97

Parsons, Talcott; Robert, F. Bales (1955): Family socialization and Interaction Process. Free Press.

Planning Budgeting and Monitoring Office (PBMO) (2004): Obafemi Awolowo University, Ile-Ife.

Piaget, J. (1932): The Moral Judgment of the child. Harcourt. Brace and World.

Rudin, M.R. (1990): Cults and Satanism NASSP Bulletin. Vol.74 No. 527 pp 46-51.

Ryan D.G. (1953) The investigation of Teacher Characteristics. The Educational Record. 34. October 371-396.

Sanford, Nevitt (1960): Self and Society. Alterton Clinical Account of the socialization Process.

Samuelson I. (1983): The Economic roles of Private Activity in E. Mannisfield Principles of Macro-economics. Readings. Issues and Cases.

Soyemi, B.O.; Jegede, O.S. (2000): Student Dictionary of Mathematics. Ode-Remo. Wiseword.

Stoodley, B. (1962): Society and Self Free Press.

Thorburn, P.; Orton, A. (1990): One More Learning Difficulty Mathematics in School. 19(3), 18-19.

Thorndike, E.L. (2000): The Principles of Teaching. Routledge and Kegan Paul Ltd. London.

Todaro, M. P. (1985): Economics for a Developing World. Longman, Singapore Publishers Ltd.

Thorp, W.H.; Harlow, F.J. (1930): Report on Technical College Organization for Nigeria. A seasonal Paper No II. Government Printers. Lagos

Udoffe, R.(1991): The Menace of Campus Cults. Chronicle. June 3.

Umo, U. C. (2001): Impact of Culture on Violence: Implications for Higher Education In Crises and Chanllenges in Higher Education in Developing Countries: A Book of Readings (eds) Akubue, A.U.; Enyi D. Nsukka.

UNESCO (2003): Education in a Multilingual World Education Position Paper.

United Nations Organization (1995): <u>Women in a Changing Global Economy</u>: World Survey on the Role of Women in Development, New York.

United Nations Development Program (UNDP) (1997) Human development Against Poverty. International Symposium of the World Bank Launch of the Human Development Report (UNDP/HDR).

United States Department of Health and Human services (2003) Substance Abuse and Mental Health Services Administration.

Von Brawn, J.; Kennedy, E. (1986): Commercialization of Subsistence Agriculture: Income and Nutritional Effects in a Developing Countries. Working Paper on Commercialization of Agriculture and Nutritional No 1 IFPRI. Washington.

Wichterick, C. (1985): Another Development with the other Sex. <u>Development and Cooperation.</u> Vol. 6.

Whitehead, A.N. (1962): <u>The Aims of Education and other Essays</u>. Ernest Benn Ltd. London.

Whitten, Lori (2005<u>) A Brief Encounter with Peer Educator can Motivate Abstinence.</u>

INDEX

978-0-595-47781-4
0-595-47781-X

www.ingramcontent.com/pod-product-compliance
Lightning Source LLC
Chambersburg PA
CBHW020411290526
45785CB00002B/514